THE SPARKING DISCIPLINE
OF CRIMINOLOGY

Society, Crime and Criminal Justice

Series Editors:

THE SPARKING DISCIPLINE
OF CRIMINOLOGY

John Braithwaite and the Construction
of Critical Social Science and Social Justice

Edited by
STEPHAN PARMENTIER, LODE WALGRAVE,
IVO AERTSEN, JEROEN MAESSCHALCK
& LETIZIA PAOLI

LEUVEN UNIVERSITY PRESS

ISBN 978 90 5867 883 6
D/ 2011 / 1869 / 27
NUR: 824
Layout: Friedemann BVBA - Hasselt

TABLE OF CONTENTS

INTRODUCTION:
CRIMINOLOGY IN SEARCH OF NEW FRONTIERS

Ivo Aertsen, Jeroen Maesschalck, Letizia Paoli,
Stephan Parmentier and Lode Walgrave

Background

On 4 February 2008 John Braithwaite received an honorary doctorate from the Catholic University of Leuven (K.U.Leuven, Belgium). By doing so, both the university and the Leuven Institute of Criminology (LINC) wished to express their deep appreciation for the crucial role that Braithwaite has played over the last decades in the development of international criminology and his relentless efforts to create links between criminology and other scientific disciplines. The ceremony was the more remarkable when taking into account that the general theme of the 2008 university-wide honorary doctorates was 'sustainable development' and that the two other foreign colleagues were heralded for their contributions to natural sciences (fisheries and food policies) and medical sciences (air pollution and lung diseases) respectively. In his honorary speech delivered on this occasion (and reproduced in this volume) Stephan Parmentier (K.U.Leuven) underscored the consecutive phases in Braithwaite's impressive academic career and situated his outstanding scientific work in the context of sustainable development in the social world.

On the same occasion the Leuven Institute of Criminology decided to organize an international colloquium under the title 'Criminology and social justice'. The reason for choosing this topic lay in the intensive and overt commitment of Braithwaite's criminological work to issues of social justice in the broad sense. His scientific engagement and expertise have consistently been imbued with a firm ethical view on humankind and society, oriented towards social justice, participative democracy, security and peace. These issues are considered of paramount importance in a world without borders but nevertheless characterized by many conflicts of different natures. Braithwaite for many years continues to be one of the most vocal leaders in committing the social sciences to the broader movement for sustainable social development.

A collection of essays

The organizational team at Leuven has compiled the most important contributions to the colloquium in this volume, which is built on two pillars. The first is a reflection on the implications of a republican theory of justice for criminology and criminal policy, whilst the second pillar relates to the role of academic criminology in today's social, political and economic environment. In addressing these two central threads the respective authors look at the work and the inspiration of this giant in criminology who is John Braithwaite, and they make frequent references to him and his work. The book consists of five chapters from well-known academics that address both aspects in various ways, and it concludes with a final reflection by John Braithwaite himself. All chapters have been written specifically for this collection and thus constitute original work.

The first carries the intriguing title 'Between evangelism and charlatanism' and is written by Lode Walgrave (K.U.Leuven). He opens the debate by reflecting on the social responsibility of criminology and other social sciences to contribute to a more livable world and a higher quality of social life. This is both possible and necessary, in his view, even if scholars in these fields may hold ideologically very different views on how such a better world can be conceived. The author first critically analyses the decline in civic engagement and mutual trust of the recent decades in Western countries, whereby the distance between governments and citizens seems to have increased. In their efforts to reduce the fear of citizens and regain their trust governments increasingly focus on crime and specifically on crime committed by marginalised individuals and groups. While acknowledging that such analysis could result in depression and immobilism, and even in cynical self-interest, Walgrave also offers some 'exit' scenarios from the deadlock. Criticizing what has been called 'embedded criminology', which operates within the limits of populism and government-defined problems, he vigorously calls for a 'socially responsible criminology' that not only informs governments but also address the general public in order to improve the public debate on crime and security issues. He advocates a balanced scientific criminology that combines strong empirical work to avoid 'evangelism', but also provides good social theory to avoid 'charlatanism'.

In the chapter 'Our sense of justice' Susanne Karstedt (Leeds University) wishes to engage with republican theory and republicanism, two concepts so central to Braithwaite's work and aiming to provide both an explanatory as well as a normative connection for restorative justice. Starting from the premise that republican theory has a firm democratic undertone and a strong foundation in egalitarian values and attitudes, her ambitious goal is to conduct an empirical test of republican theory as a normative theory of justice. To do so, she has carefully conducted two studies based on extensive statistical information from various databases covering 67 countries in the world: the first empirical study focuses on the relationships between the values of non-interference in private life and equality before the law on the one hand and degrees of punishment on the other hand; the second study focuses on the relationships between egalitarian values and state violence. Karstedt concludes that countries where values of individual autonomy and individual freedom are dominant, as well as countries with high levels of egalitarianism values, display lower imprisonment rates and less harsh punishment regimes than countries with less emphasis on individual autonomy and higher levels of authoritarian or non-egalitarian values. She argues that these results underscore the importance of equality as the core value of Braithwaite's republican theory of justice and indicate that the said theory is not merely 'utopian' but can be demonstrated in a 'tangible fashion'.

The social role of academic criminology, the second major strand in the book, is broached in the chapter 'Why criminology needs outsiders' by Tom Daems (K.U.Leuven). 'Outsiders' in his understanding refer to the limited number of criminologists who invite others to take distance from their daily work and raise uncommon issues, with a view of promoting self-awareness for the community of criminologists and for criminology as a discipline. Daems then goes on to discuss the important contributions of five such outsiders who nevertheless continue to be embraced by the criminological family: Stan Cohen, Nils Christie, Louk Hulsman, David Garland and John Braithwaite. In varying degrees they have tried to overcome the power/knowledge connection that Foucault criticized in relation to criminology and criminal policy. Through examples from the sociology of punishment and from restorative justice research Daems meticulously argues and demonstrates how easily criminological researchers get stuck in their traditional straight-jackets of assumptions, concepts and conclusions. This leads him to conclude that uncomfortable questions from outsiders are of paramount importance in safeguarding and developing the critical core of the criminological activity.

The next chapter 'Braithwaite, criminology and the debate on public social science' takes the discussion one step further into the larger world of social sciences and offers a very thoughtful account from a 'sociology of science' viewpoint. The starting point of Ian Loader (Oxford University) and Richard

Sparks (University of Edinburgh) is to rethink the character and scope of contemporary social science work on crime, justice and public policy, with a view of understanding what it means to *apply* criminological knowledge or *influence* criminal policy. First, they discuss the predicaments of criminology today and note that many authors speak of the "successful failure" of criminology, booming as it is in professional terms but, simultaneously, losing its connection with governmental crime policies and with the general public. In order to gain deeper insight into the reasons of the successful failure paradox, as well as the consequences it entails, they investigate similar debates in adjacent fields like sociology and argue that the problems extend to social sciences as a whole. Drawing on Braithwaite's strong arguments for intellectual pluralism and his living example to build a public social science "with more tents and fewer buildings" the authors embark upon an intriguing journey to 're-think' the promise of criminology as part of the social sciences. They identify and critically analyse three current strands, 'hyper-specialisation', 'legislative utterance' and 'dissolution'. Rather than embracing any of these, Loader and Sparks make a convincing plea for another approach, namely an in-depth sociological enquiry into the field of criminological knowledge production itself. Their chapter ends with laying out the signposts of such historical-hermeneutical investigation of criminology to be undertaken in the future.

In reply to the previous chapter, Bart Pattyn (K.U.Leuven) raises the provocative question 'Why research cannot but be trans-disciplinary in complex matters of ethos and justice', which is also the title of his contribution to the book. The aim is to figure out how ethics can be involved in a trans-disciplinary reflection on social control, shame and reintegration, which constitute direct references to the core concepts developed by Braithwaite. Pattyn first provides an interesting analysis of how the 'politics of specialization' have become the standard in academia. This has led many researchers to limit their expertise to very small and specific topics, partly out of scrupulousness to be in full control of their field of expertise, but also because it provides more security to be part of a small self-referential group when academic evaluations come around. The risk is that many academics are cut off from other fields and lack the type of contingent knowledge to explain complex phenomena. The author then argues why the work of Braithwaite and Pettit on 'dominion' and restorative justice offers new breathing space by cutting across several academic disciplines, like ethics, law, communication, psychology, etc. Using the concept of 'ethos', he engages in a highly enlightening ethical reflection on how to create respect for dominion and argues in favour of positive projects to such end. This 'alternative ethos' cannot only strengthen the practice of restorative justice conferences where victims and offenders encounter each other, but it can also pave the way for genuine trans-disciplinary research about the outside world that remains intertwined.

The sixth and final chapter is from the hand of the master himself. Indeed, John Braithwaite, the person whose work and life has inspired so many criminologists and social scientists graciously agreed to write a concluding piece for this book. For sure, he has formulated extensive and insightful comments to the preceding chapters in the book. But he also reaches far beyond this intent and has written a very personal, self-standing and original piece on the challenges and future directions for criminology. His chapter 'Opportunities and dangers of capitalist criminology' starts with the provoking argument that criminology has brought a lot of good to the world but that its evolution is very doubtful. The reason for the latter lies in the nature of "regulatory capitalism" that has not only influenced crime control industries all over the world through the simultaneous trends of privatization and state interventionism, but also has a strong impact on teaching and research in criminology. One manifestation is the new forms of "regulatory metrics" by business and the professional academy, forcing criminologists like other (social) scientists to publish in English-speaking international journals with high prestige and/or high impact factors rather than in places where the most relevant people will engage with their work. By doing so, Western universities have become "careerist places where inmates keep their heads down and seek to get ahead in the education market". Braithwaite fulminates against "the mindless pursuit of quantitative indicators of excellence" because they do not push scientists to exploring innovative and challenging ideas but on the contrary, and inevitably, promote certainty and stagnation of the field. His vision is one of constructing alternatives to the dominant Anglo-Saxon quantitative model, by looking at new visions of crime and criminology and new indicators of excellence in Asia and other parts of the world. To break away from the deadlock and to bridge the traditional divide between normative and explanatory theory in social life, criminology has to transform itself into "sparking criminology". This also includes reinvigorating the role of universities as places of critical thought and action that may run counter the well-established views of academic, social, political and economic elites. Only by following this path and by sparking transformative projects across disciplines, Braithwaite argues, criminology is able to break away from the iron logic of regulatory capitalism and can redeem our failing universities.

The chapter by Braithwaite is followed by a selection of his publications between 1979 and 2010. The list testifies of his most impressive academic production as well as of the superb quality of his scholarship.

To conclude

The above makes clear that this collection of essays does not lead to fixed, let alone uniform, conclusions; that was not its intention, nor would it be possible given the rich and diverging sets of ideas advanced here. At the same time, there is no doubt that the book contains many new ideas around issues of social justice and sustainable development that are thought-provoking and therefore worthy of further study. Moreover, the book does not only make an interesting read but also appeals to concrete action, both examples that Braithwaite himself has set so successfully throughout his career.

This collection is intended for a wide readership, including academics and researchers, graduate students, policy-makers, civil servants, civil society actors and the media working in the fields of criminology, restorative justice and social regulation. These readers are by no means limited to Europe, but can easily extend to other countries and continents, even to the entire globe.

LAUDATIO FOR JOHN BRAITHWAITE
Delivered at the K.U.Leuven on 4 February 2008

STEPHAN PARMENTIER

Your Eminence,
Rector,
Your Excellencies,
Dear Colleagues,
Ladies and Gentlemen,

What do restorative justice, financial regulation and peacebuilding in post-conflict societies have in common? Most observers will be puzzled by this quiz-like question and will resort to sophisticated search engines on the World Wide Web to find an answer. For all us today, however, the answer is a very simple one, for the three topics mentioned have all been studied *in extenso* and with immense depth and great skill by our *doctor honoris causa-to-be*, Professor John Braithwaite.

"The most cited author" in international criminological journals during the 1990s, "one of the most influential criminologists of our time", and "the new Durkheim", are merely some of the many epithets with which John Braithwaite has been heralded in the social sciences. He can, without further ado, be regarded as an intellectual giant who belongs to the absolute world top, and continues to shape this very world top from day to day.

His career spans more than thirty years that can roughly be subdivided into three main periods. Starting his scientific writings at the age of 24 years, the young Braithwaite is immediately drawn to study all aspects of crime and ethically inspired responses to them. His early publications back in the 1970s on corporate crime and corruption gradually lead him to focus on the overarching problem of how to regulate individual corporations and the world of business at large.

The major breakthrough comes in 1989 with the book *Crime, Shame and Reintegration*, which introduces the concept of "re-integrative shaming". This implies that persons having committed a criminal offence – whether petty or serious – can be "shamed" for their absence of conformity with the existing rules, but should always be given the possibility to "reintegrate" themselves into ordinary life of mainstream society. Braithwaite shows how "re-integrative shaming" is an inclusive approach to deal with crime, as well as a very powerful mechanism to respect the dignity of all human beings – offenders and victims alike – and to prevent crime in the long run. "Disintegrative shaming" as an exclusive approach, on the other hand, in his view mostly leads to stigmatisation, feelings of anger and revenge, and further deviance. These ideas are developed further in *Not Just Deserts. A Republican Theory of Criminal Justice* (with Pettit, Clarendon Press, 1990). Both authors make a strong plea for criminal law and criminal justice systems that are more participative for all parties involved, and focus on the preservation of "dominion", a unique combination of rights and freedoms of modern society as well as the certainty that these will be upheld.

The powerful theoretical vision underlying both works has profoundly influenced and renewed the discipline of criminology over the past 20 years. This took place in particular in relationship to the theory and practice of restorative justice in which offenders and victims, and other parties in a conflict, are brought together to deal with the aftermath of a criminal act and to work together towards repairing the harm inflicted. Many of these ideas have been picked up and further developed by academic and criminal justice institutions all over all globe, and particularly in Belgium that has established itself as a forerunner in this field over the past decade. Brief reference can be made here to the pioneering work of Leuven based academic networks such as the "International Network for Research on Restorative Justice for Juveniles" and the "European Forum for Restorative Justice", as well as the Leuven Public Prosecutor's Service that first allowed victim-offender mediation for more serious crimes and the Ministry of Justice that introduced restorative justice in all Belgian prisons. Years later, at the turn of the millennium, international institutions such as the European Union and the United Nations have also discovered the powerful message of restorative justice and have embraced its potential.

As a truly innovative thinker, however, John Braithwaite cannot be caged in one box and is always challenging new fields for his concepts and theories to be applied. At the turn of the century another milestone publication, *Restorative Justice and Responsive Regulation* (Oxford University Press, 2002), allows him to view restorative justice as a multiple and multi-layered concept that ranges from the micro level of individual encounters up to the macro level of states and further. Hence the challenge to investigate the possibilities and limits of restorative justice and responsive regulation in fields far beyond traditional crime and criminology, reaching deep into the areas of political science, sociology and economics. His books *Global Business Regulation* (with P. Drahos, Cambridge University Press, 2000) and *Markets in Vice, Markets in Virtue* (Oxford University Press, 2005) tackle very sensitive topics, such as the extreme hardship inflicted by ruthless capitalism in many parts of the world, and do explore new avenues for peaceful, just and inclusive development. The same holds true with his worldwide and ambitious project on *Peace-building and Responsive Governance* since 2006 that studies the dynamics of peace-building after violent conflicts through 48 case-studies over a twenty-year period.

Besides being a builder of bridges between various disciplines, and between theoretical and empirical approaches, professor Braithwaite is also a builder of networks. Back in 2001 he set up the *Regulatory Institutions Network (Regnet)* at the Research School of Social Sciences in Canberra. In its short life time, this truly global network of institutions, practitioners and academics has gained worldwide recognition for its high-quality research on regulation issues in fields as diverse as peace building, social justice, human rights and sustainable development. Braithwaite is also lauded for his leadership to commit the social sciences to an ethical approach towards issues of social justice, participative democracy, human rights and world peace.

Given these extensive qualifications, it is both amazing and laudable that John Braithwaite has managed to remain a very warm and charming person, open to all and everyone without distinction, gifted with a very down-under Australian sense of wit and humour, and above all, with a 'non-ego' difficult to match in our current competitive world.

Over the past decade, John Braithwaite has closely worked together with several members of the almost 80-years old Leuven Institute of Criminology, and notably with emeritus professor Lode Walgrave, and he and his colleagues have paid several pleasant visits to our university. Because of his impressive career, his paramount scientific contribution to the social sciences and his powerful ethical vision, the whole team of our Criminology Institute and the Faculty of Law have enthusiastically supported the candidacy of Braithwaite, also in view of further strengthening the mutual cooperation between Leuven and Canberra. The honorary university degree for John Braithwaite is particularly well taken in the context of this year's central theme of "Sustainable Development", since this encompasses more than clean water and clean air, and it entails more than the survival of endangered species and cultural practices. Sustainable development also deeply refers to relationships in the social world that deal with peace, social justice and inclusive citizenship, relationships that need to be restored or to be built up from scratch, relationships between individual people as well as at the collective level of groups, nations and the international community at large. Sustainable development is indeed a multi-dimensional reality as much as a concept, and poses enormous challenges for all regions of today's global village, including our own multicultural society.

For all these reasons, I ask you, honoured Rector, on the recommendation of the Academic Council, to grant the honorary doctorate of the Katholieke Universiteit Leuven to Professor John Braithwaite.

BETWEEN EVANGELISM AND CHARLATANISM: REFLECTIONS ON THE SOCIAL RESPONSIBILITY OF CRIMINOLOGY AND OTHER SOCIAL SCIENCES[1]

LODE WALGRAVE

Introduction

Some scientists behave like chickens. Chickens lay their egg without any concern about how it will be used. Whether it will be used for an omelette, be boiled hard, scrambled, laid out to hatch or simply thrown away, chickens do not care. Likewise, some scientists produce their 'truth', lay their 'egg of knowledge', and do not worry about how it will be used. Whether it is applied to produce more energy or a bomb, to cure people or to torture them more efficiently, to improve living conditions for all or to increase individual profits of the rich, to increase understanding of people in trouble or to provide new labels to justify their social exclusion – these scientists do not consider it as their business. Their only mission, they claim, is to produce knowledge. Just as the chicken's mission is to produce eggs.

I view the mission of scientists as higher than laying eggs. It is not because they are members of the scientific community that scientists stop being members of the human community as a whole. As such, we may expect that they care about the way their work is integrated in social practice. Scientists must be aware of their social ethical responsibility and reflect on how their activity may contribute, directly or indirectly, to a more livable world and a higher quality of social life, even if they may hold ideologically very different views on how this better world is to be conceived.

Current developments, imbued with crime, (un)safety and justice concerns, confront criminology, more than before, with the necessity to reflect on its social responsibility.

---

[1]   This chapter is largely inspired by Chapter Six 'Democracy, Criminology and Restorative Justice', in L. Walgrave (2008) *Restorative Justice, Self-Interest and Responsible Citizenship*, Cullompton, UK: Willan Publishing.

Declining quality of Western democracies and penal populism

The relations between global socio-economic change, existential fear, politics in crime and justice issues, and the decline of participatory democracy have been the subject of many debates and publications.[2] I will not discuss the variations on this theme here, but present briefly what I make of it.

Putnam (2000) gives a compelling account of the decline of social capital, "connections among individuals - social networks and the norms of reciprocity and trustworthiness that arise from them" (ibid.: 19), in the United States. "Politics without social capital is politics at a distance" (ibid.: 341). Civic participation in democracy fades away.

The decline in civic engagement and in mutual trust seems to be a Western phenomenon of recent decades. The distance between governments and citizens is increasing, yielding a democratic deficit and growing discontent of citizens. Common sense bottom-up input from everyday life gets lost and gives way to extremist, technocratic or professionalised options and decisions, making participation and control from the grassroots still more difficult.

It is surprising that Putnam, documenting the loss of social capital in a number of realms of social and economic life, does not include dynamics in the field of crime, justice and safety. If he had done so, he would have seen that perception of more crime and less safety is probably the nucleus of infection which gradually contaminates the overall quality of social life, civic commitment and democracy. And the basis for the deterioration of the perception of crime, justice and safety is capitalist globalisation.

Uncertainty and risk

In my view, it all began at the end of the 1960s. What were originally student protests against concrete local and global policy issues gradually broadened to contest the organisation of societies and the cultural hegemony as a whole. From demonstrating against war and warmongering governments, they began

---

[2]   As, for example, in (the contributions in) Wacquant (1999), Young (1999), Baumann (2000), Garland & Sparks (2000), Karstedt & Bussman (2000), Garland (1996 and 2001), Stenson & Sullivan (2001), Crawford (2002), Hughes & Edwards (2002), Wood & Dupont (2006), and many others.

to attack all political and moral authority. Bourgeois society was reproached as oppressing the free deployment of individuals in all aspects of life.

The movement also penetrated developments in social sciences, especially those dealing with deviance. "Anti-psychiatrists" stigmatised traditional clinical sciences as being one-sidedly used and ideologically misused in order to attribute deviance to individual deficiencies. Radical and critical criminology saw crime as a normal response to an abnormal and unjust world and to its institutional interventions (as for example in Taylor, Walton & Young 1973).

The movement was very influential. Within a decade, its ideas had seeped into mainstream culture, politics and the messages of moral authorities. It held the seeds of the so-called post-modernist and deconstructivist philosophy, announcing the end of the great religious, moral, nationalist stories, deconstructing the authority of churches and governments. People had to construct their own lives and to make decisions on the basis of their own moral code. It grounded what Boutellier (2005) calls optimistically cultural "vitality", an unprecedented experience of freedom.

However, what was meant to be an emancipating movement actually detached people from a solid structure, and moral and cultural frames. Appeals for greater responsibility of the individual led to selfish, hedonistic attitudes and a loss of binding elements in social life, causing cultural anxiety and uncertainty. This was not helped by the explosion of mass media – first television and later internet – which brought cultural globalisation. Today, we are confronted with strange lifestyles, different morals, and provocative opinions that challenge our own frame of moral, cultural and political beliefs, evidence and standards. The solid ground of our life is affected.

In the same period, capitalist globalisation boosted the financial and economic power of multinational enterprises, beyond the power of governments (Baumann 2000). Finances move to where the most profit can be made. Multinational capitalist interest groups relocate investments; play the social models in different countries off against each other to keep down wages, social advantages and certainties; move employment to regions where exploitation of labour forces is easier and more beneficial; manipulate the prices of crucial raw materials; destroy the environment; even promote war or peace. Moreover, legal and illegal immigrants, seeking some crumbs of western wealth, add to the confrontation with cultural heterogeneity and the breakdown of the world with its familiar stakes and predictabilities.

The more capitalist interests are spread worldwide the less local governments are able to control the basic conditions on which to develop their social, economic, welfare and cultural policy. On the contrary, governments have to accommodate capitalist interests to keep the economy going, which is needed to get the means for their policy. And so, capitalist globalisation tightens its grip on the world. Global economic, social and safety developments, with direct impact on citizens' living conditions and opportunities, have far transcended the decision margins of individual governments. Impotent to control the capitalist forces, governments submit their citizens to the market rhetorics through a discourse of responsibilisation. It is up to the citizens themselves to find their way around the mushrooming opportunities and offers, including the risks of being defrauded or cheated; they are primarily responsible for their own security. It leaves the citizens alone with their fear of being misled and misused (Karstedt & Farrall 2004).

Both the cultural and moral fluidity and the socio-economic uncertainty are the basis for the overall *Unsicherheit* (Baumann 2000b: 137), an existential feeling of insecurity that affects all aspects of life – our relationships, our socio-economic position, our environment, our food, our health. We are living in an area of "liquid modernity" (Baumann 2000b), in which nothing is fixed and nothing is predictable.

In principle, uncertainty is not necessarily negative. It can create new opportunities to break through the old rigid structures. This is the case for the few best-off in societies, who profit from the deregulation of the markets. The best off in society indeed have the power to 'steer the boat on the lake of liquid modernity'. Most citizens, however, are happy that they caught the boat (and enjoy their part of "vitality"), but are powerless to steer it. They row where the powerful tell them to row, but are uncertain about where that will bring them. Finally, those who missed the boat have to swim on their own, or drown.

The uncertainty is perceived as risk (Beck 1992, Giddens 1998). Also in Boutellier's optimistic account, the increased freedom unavoidably leads to an obsession with safety. It is likely that, objectively speaking, risks have not increased. We are currently, more than ever, able to prevent natural disasters or to control many of their consequences; medical care can cure more health problems than ever before, and has made our lives longer and more comfortable; we are pampered by "*des protections civiles*", as guaranteed through legal rights, and by "*des protections sociales*", as provided by the social system (Castel 2003). But we are very sensitive now to new 'humanly manufactured uncertainty', such as terrorism, global warming, unemployment, disrupted relations, dangerous traffic and 'predatory criminals' (Stenson 2001). In the words of Lianos and Douglas (2000: 110-111), "[D]angerization is the tendency to perceive and analyse the world through categories of menace. It leads to continuous detection of threats and assessment of adverse probabilities, to the prevalence of defensive perceptions over optimistic ones and to the dominance of fear and anxiety over ambition and desire".

Consumer democracy

What can citizens do? Many citizens are aware of their powerlessness and understand that their governments have, at best, only marginal impact on social and political developments. Governments try to cope with globality and complexity by appealing increasingly to the expertise of economists, jurists, engineers (and criminologists). It creates a playground for self-interested lobbying by powerful groups in back rooms, which mostly results in the capitalist market being presented as a natural thing that cannot be avoided, so that the labour market must become more flexible, the wages of employees lower, and the income for capitalist employers higher.

Technical expertise is beyond the understanding and control of citizens, and thus increases still more the distance between citizens and their governments. The more citizens lose their grip, directly and indirectly, on the conditions of their existence the more they find it impossible to contribute significantly to their own conditions of life, and the more they reduce their social commitment. In Putnam's words (2000), social capital is shrinking. Many citizens no longer take responsibility for the quality of social life. They try to hide away from insecurity by withdrawing into fortresses of self-interest and retreating into a post-modern re-construction of self-serving norms and values. "Deciding what is illegal, or simply unfair or unethical, becomes idiosyncratic and personalised" (Kardstedt & Farrall 2007: 5). Social life is characterised by "market anomie …an increasing erosion of legal norms, moral standards and trust, culminating in a climate of mutual suspicion and rampant moral cynicism" (ibid.).

The democratic game has lost a great deal of its relevance for citizens' lives. It is hollowed out as a kind of shadow play. Elections are rituals with almost ornamental issues only, looked at like sports events. "What does it matter … if the crucial decisions that affect their destiny are no longer being made by democratic government at all?" (Barber 2003: xiii).

Indifference in democratic life is complemented by consumption of democratic institutions. Citizens consider the social institutions and the law as consumers do. They want value for their tax money. They try to get the most possible benefits at the lowest possible price. Social institutions are consumed: rights and institutional offers are exploited to the full and obligations are avoided or circumvented as far as possible, even if this leads to so-called "everyday crimes of the middle classes" (Karstedt & Farrall 2007). "Freedom becomes indistinguishable from selfishness, and is corrupted from within by apathy, alienation, and anomie; equality is reduced to market exchangeability and divorced from its necessary familial and social context; happiness is measured by material gratification to the detriment of the spirit" (Barber 2003: 24). In electoral campaigns profits are offered as bargains, and many citizens behave like bargain hunters: they do not vote for the candidate who proposes the best option for social life but for the one who is expected to defend best their own selfish interests. Democracy becomes a consumer democracy, an arena of struggle for the maximum possible consumption of rights and opportunities at the lowest possible price.

Penal populism

What can governments do? In the consumerist democracy governments must deliver goods in a hold between three spheres of interest: (1) the demands of the capitalist groups, which governments need to humour to maintain an attractive investment climate and to keep the economy going; (2) the pressure of consumerist citizens, who want to maximize their share of economic benefits and to consume the maximum possible of the available offers of goods and social institutions; (3) the needs of those who have 'missed the boat' and are living in poverty at the margins of society. They risk drowning.

To obtain the means for producing their goods (economic facilities, social, educational, welfare and culture policy), governments must please the capitalists; to be re-elected, they must please the mainstream consumerist citizens. A compromise between these two spheres of interest is possible. But saving the drowning people is more complicated. As globalisation has moved much unskilled work to the Third World unemployment of the unskilled in Western societies is creating a growing underclass, without realistic prospects for integration in economic and social life. Governments can either let them drown, which would shock the moral values of a considerable proportion of the mainstream voters (as we shall see, ethics are not completely lost) and would be very risky for public safety (it pollutes the lake [3]); or they can give the 'swimmers' a hand to get on board, which would cost money (to the detriment of the first two groups) and delay the boat.

Delivering existential safety by focusing on the fundamental causes of the *Unsicherheit* among citizens and their cynical defensive attitudes is beyond governments' capacity. But doing nothing is not an option either. And so governments focus on crime, advanced as the main cause of fear. But they focus selectively on the crime committed by the marginalised, those without defence against negative stereotyping. It has become a central issue in national politics. Because "unpredictable 'market forces' ... are far beyond the reach of ... territory bound governments" (Baumann 2000: 36), those governments address local crime and safety problems. For the impotent governments, "doing something, or be seen to be doing something, about fighting the crime which threatens personal safety is a realistic option – and one containing a lot of electoral potential" (ibid.).

A focus on crime projects the existential anxiety onto concrete objects, which creates the illusion that the problems can be tackled. The message: "we know what the problem is, we know how to tackle it, and we can do it" is a more comforting and electorally rewarding message than admitting that "all we can do is tinker a bit at the margins of the problem, but we are unable to change the causes of your fundamental uncertainty and anxiety".

The media fuel anxiety and focus on crime topics (Roberts e.a. 2003). As commercial enterprises, they have subjugated their overt aim of informing the public to their actual objective, which is to make profits for their owners. The media want to sell their products, and they therefore produce popular, smoothly receivable messages. Following the consumerist mood in the public, they amplify the pursuit of easily accessible safety. Complicated reality is reduced in simplistic articles. Juicy stories are more important than good and balanced information. Media coverage of crime and justice issues is an essential actor in what Kutchinsky (1979) called the "crime carousel", a complex of mutually strengthening social forces, activated by media, interest groups of professionals, right-wing politicians, and the private security industry, which together contribute to the myth of an ever-increasing and ever-more violent crime wave, threatening our lives and property, and those of our loved ones. The myth is currently presented as indisputable fact, in as much as those who express doubts about it are outcast (Kappeler, Blumberg and Potter 2000).

---

[3]   Baumann (2004) speaks of "wasted lives". If you drop waste in a lake, it pollutes the lake.

All this feeds the penal populism of governments. Consumerist democracy runs on populism. Populism follows the superficial sentiments of the population, aiming at immediate comfort and benefits, without caring about adequate information and without ethical reflections. Populist politicians, for example, promise fewer taxes but do not balance this with realistic plans for savings, nor do they care about the consequences for those who are hurt by the savings. They lash out at immigrants, but do not have feasible, ethically well thought-out proposals to deal with immigration. They advertise more punishment, but do not say what would be the consequences for the punished and do not advance any good idea about the effects of more punishment on public safety. Populism has a narrow perspective on short-term benefits in selfish terms, because of its lack of information and ethical reflection. It is barefaced consumerism of social institutions, a travesty of democracy.[4]

"Penal populism ... is defined ... as a punishment policy developed primarily for its anticipated popularity" (Roberts e.a. 2003: 64-65). "A populist penal agenda emerges ... from the preferences of political 'consumers' – the electorate" (id.: 66). And the consumerist citizens' request is that the authorities deliver total security at the lowest possible price. They demand a safe environment in which to do their business undisturbed, and enjoy their comfort unhampered. The means that are used for this end do not matter, as long as the investment in terms of cost and civic commitment is the lowest possible. Decreasing solidarity and shrinking civic commitment lead to a shift from concern for social problems and poverty to 'dangerisation' and criminalising of the poor (Wacquant 1999, Young 1999). Hence the punitive option, because it does not ask uncomfortable questions about the living conditions of those punished. Incapacitation delivers more immediate security than does social work.

The penal populism of governments, however, does not create more security (Buruma 2005). On the contrary, "the expansion of security ... promises reassurance but in fact increases anxiety...." (Zedner 2003: 157). Paradoxically, because the citizens' need for safety is insatiable, the 'war against crime and incivilities' demonstrates the actual incapacity of governments to satisfy the consumerist citizens' demands. On the contrary, "[T]he unfulfillable promises of a crime-free society, the unwarranted promises to victims, the installing of

---

[4] I am not pleading for the opposite of populism, namely elitism that shows disdain for emotions in the public. Emotions and self-interested views are crucial in a good working democracy but it is equally crucial that information and ethical debates give these emotions a more pondered and – hopefully – a more constructive content.

fear: these are all palpable effects of the populists' discourse on punishment" (Daems 2007: 24). Hence the disenchantment with democratic institutions increases (Stenson & Edwards 2001), and extreme right authoritarian politics become more and more attractive.

Extension: is there more crime?

The preceding paragraphs focused on the perception that crime has raised dramatically, but left unanswered the question whether there is actually more crime. I simply don't know and I pretend that nobody can. The available figures are not unambiguous and their value for measuring real crime is doubtful.

Based on theory we might suspect, however, that more crime is committed than before at several levels of society. The increasing power of the captains of capitalism to the detriment of national governments may have tipped the control balance (Tittle 1995) so that these captains are increasingly able to control their controllers and find opportunities to commit white collar crime at a large scale. The loss of social commitment and the raise of selfish consumerism may provoke more middle class crime (as suggested by Karstedt and Farall 2007). Global social economic developments, immigration and local consumerism increase dualisation in society, increasing the risk of more crime by the socially excluded; they probably commit more crime to survive, or as a way of coping with the anomie they are living in (Merton 1938, Messner and Rosenfeld 1994). Moreover, "[they] have nothing to lose: they have 'fallen below the threshold of deterrence'" (O'Malley 2006: 220).

The criminal justice paradox (Boutellier 1996) is that the system is less able to cope with this raising and changing crime phenomenon, while the appeal to it is unrealistically great. It adds to the discontent with social institutions and the tendency for self-oriented consumerism.

Submitting welfare work to safety conditions

The evolution described so far is not a simple downward spiral, leading to complete cynical selfishness and punitiveness. While the consumerist tendency is gaining considerable support in the public mentality, it is curbed and corrected. As humans, mainstream citizens continue to be moved by a fundamental interhuman sympathy, especially in their relation to weak and the vulnerable.[5] Many are still driven by socio-ethical reflections and do feel solidarity.

How can the pursuit of safety be combined with some support for the poor? "How to include the 'truly disadvantaged' minority without alienating the contented majority who constitute the political base of support for parties…" (Stenson & Edwards 2001: 70)? The answer is to include welfare rhetorics in security policy, as in the British 'third way', or in the 'integrative prevention-strategies' on the European continent (Hebberecht & Sack 1997, Goris 2001). Police forces and welfare workers are supposed to work together in local community development and to enhance reintegration of families and young people at risk, as a way to promote safety for all. It is the ideal compromise for governments that are trying to restore their legitimacy by fighting crime, but still want to keep an ethical flavour in their policy. Conditional support for the marginalized is told to enhance their motivation to behave in an orderly way, and hence also public safety. Combining "tough on crime" with being "tough on the causes of crime" seems to satisfy both the safety-seeking and the social ethical citizen. Social work and community development in deprived neighbourhoods, youth work, monitoring of school careers of young people at risk, observation of parenting performance in families – all can be part of 'progressive' welfare schemes, but all can be inserted into safety policy as well.

And the latter is what mostly happens. The submission of welfare work to the security rationale in fact constitutes a betrayal of the original social ethical motives of welfare work. Welfare work was originally driven by a genuine ethical solidarity with the poor and other people in trouble, but it is now reframed as a means of enhancing safety for the better-off. People in trouble are not recognized as needing help but as possible risks for others. Support for their welfare and integration is submitted to the condition of not disturbing the well integrated citizens. It is a way of controlling and disciplining the poor and marginalised, under the threat of greater punitiveness just described. Solidarity with the poor and marginalised is subversively replaced by calculation at the service of the rich and the well integrated citizens.

---

[5]   I cannot expand on this human sympathy issue here, but see my Chapter Three in Walgrave (2008).

Social sciences and criminology as democratic forces

If the story would end here the only perspective would be capitalist forces further enslaving people. The shortage of possible "exit scenarios" (Daems 2007) would generate depression and immobilism, or cynical and pure self-interest in an increasingly consumerist democracy. But exits there are. The social ethical motives of citizens and groups are not completely overwhelmed by consumerism. Countervailing forces are based on interhuman sympathy and the ethical forces it engenders. They find their way in civil society among conscious citizens and enlightened politicians, as can be observed in the resistance against war, the rebellion against purely capitalist globalization, the civic actions to curb global warming, and the voluntary commitments in local and international NGOs. Inspiring pieces of art bear witness to hope and the rejection of war. Schiller's *Alle Menschen werden Brüder*, the movement on these words in Beethoven's ninth symphony, and Picasso's *Guernica* are stronger appeals to keep hope and reject the atrocities humans do to each other than any rational analysis. Roman Polanski's movie *The Pianist* is a deeply touching witness that, even during the darkest days of persecution and dehumanization as in Second World War Warszawa, Chopin's Mazurka can provoke a spark of recognition and human sympathy. Social sciences make critical studies of macro-social developments and warn of the human and social disasters they may produce.

All these expressions are inspired by a common intuition. They "reject the banal, neo-liberal tendency to view the human subject in narrowly economic terms as a consumer/non-consumer or wealth creator/drone" (Stenson 2001: 24). They do not see individual profits as the basic drive in society. Rather, they are motivated by a desire for social life based on social justice and respect for pluralism, driven by solidarity and individual active responsibility. Utopian models of such societies are presented by social political sciences and social ethical philosophies. They are beacons for those who reflect on the future of our global community, and they offer visions for a scientific approach to concrete social problems.

Social sciences are not objective

Social sciences have a special role to play in the development of these countervailing forces. This is not to say that social sciences produce objective knowledge from which to deduce irrefutable political options. Social sciences operate in the real world, with a plethora of variations in situations, individual life courses, personalities, experiences, influences, motivations and prospects, where the objects of study are humans with needs and rights (and, some will say, a free will). I argue that scientific research –fatally- cannot but isolate only a part of this complex world and reduce it to some measurable dimensions and variables. It is oriented by concepts and theories which are social constructions, not objective data, and by hypotheses, which are inspired by – hopefully – original personal views; scientific research designs a research methodology, constructs variables and makes instruments to measure these variables, which are at their best creations by good scientists, acceptable by the scientific community; the collected data are processed to draw conclusions, and we must hope that this is done with original personal insight of an intelligent scientist. This pathway is not at all pre-ordained by 'the objective reality' or 'objective facts'.

Sciences cannot be objective, because they are carried out by subjective humans. *A fortiori*, social sciences cannot be objective because they study human subjects. Even the most complicated and admirable statistical arabesques cannot prevent the pathway of social sciences being paved with subjective inputs, which at their best lead to intersubjective constructions, transcending the purely subjective intuitions and suspicions of the researcher, being (provisionally) accepted as 'knowledge' by the scientific community and other 'consumers' of the results.

Yet, social scientists cannot give up the ultimate ambition. If they did not continue trying to approach objectivity, they would run the risk of sinking into impressionist intuitive statements only, without a real added value. That is why adequate scientific methodology is crucially important. Methodology is meant to channel the researcher's intuitions and suspicions through a systematic and controllable procedure of thinking and data collection: a well considered, open problem analysis based on the knowledge available, and a step-by-step account of all moves in the process of constructing data and drawing conclusions. Results and views based on good scientific research are systematically investigated, contextualized and controllable. They yield data and views that transcend the more limited, short-term oriented and biased views that prevail among the uninformed public, electorally vulnerable politicians and practitioners who are guided by interest.

The added value of scientific research lies not in delivering objective grounds for decision-making, but in its "responsible speech", taking "great care to distinguish – in a fashion clear and visible to anybody – between the statements corroborated by available evidence and such propositions as can only claim the status of a provisional, untested guess" (Baumann 1990: 12, quoted in Daems 2007: 438).

Science, and *a fortiori* social science, is caught in an irresolvable tension of the continuous pursuit of objective facts, while being capable only of discovering subjectively what is "out there". Consequently, scientific research is not only dictated by methodology and facts, but also by choices and options to be taken. It confronts criminology with its social responsibilities.

The criminological straddle

The populist obsession with crime and (un)safety and the penal populist response to it by governments force criminology in a difficult straddle. Cynically, the increasing anxiety and the focus on crime as the main cause are excellent boosts for criminology-as-business. Governments commission research and hire criminological expertise; swelling labour markets for criminologists and media attention to crime attract more and more criminology students; universities invest in profitable criminology programmes. All over the world, institutes for education in criminology and for criminological research emerge. Research is expanding and methodological quality is improving. New criminological journals are launched.

At the same time, however, criminologists deplore their loss of influence on policy-making (Haggerty 2004, Chancer & McLaughlin 2007). Indeed, it looks like a paradox that criminology is currently a flourishing business, in an epoch characterized by penal populism taking over criminal policy. What was commonly accepted in, say, the 1980s as a patrimony of criminology-based knowledge on crime and adequate crime policy seems to have been swept away in two decades by poorly thought-out, short-term-oriented punitiveness.

It is possible that global developments have modified crime problems intrinsically so deeply that the earlier criminology has lost (part of) its relevance. Capitalist globalization, mass consumption, migration and attempts to keep them under control, internet, the penetration of world conflicts in daily life through (threats of) terrorism, all these and other phenomena go far beyond the scope of earlier criminology.

But that cannot explain it all. Traditional criminality still exists, and it is tackled also much harder than before. Prisons are not full of 'new' criminals, such as international business criminals, human traffickers or terrorists, but are still populated mainly by 'old fashioned' robbers, burglars, street fighters and violent husbands. Obviously, the earlier criminological problem statements still apply, but the then conceived solutions seem too distant from the penal populist climate, and have lost attractiveness for electorally vulnerable politicians.

How must criminology cope with this problematic situation? Several positions can be advanced (Chancer & McLaughlin 2007).

Opting for an "objective" scientific criminology

Some attribute the loss of criminological influence to the ideological bias in the criminological theories and the methodological inaccuracy of criminological research. In their view criminology must go more for the "scientific method, with its emphasis on unbiased empirical research" (Farrington 1991: 32). Only strict scientific criminology, even a kind of "experimental criminology" (Sherman 2005), is the best way to regain credibility.

It is not an evident option. While the quality of methodology is of course crucial for the credibility of all intellectual activities claiming to be scientific, it is equally crucial to remain modest about the status of the knowledge that social science can achieve. As just argued, even the most rigid methodological approaches cannot deliver irrefutable objective knowledge.

The tradition of the *What Works* meta-analyses, for example, offers critical surveys of outcomes that transcend the purely subjective intuitions and suspicions of scientists and practitioners. Such surveys can serve as provisional platforms of knowledge for common reflection and action. But, contrary to what the expression "evidence-based" suggests, *What Works* cannot indicate which treatment or prevention programmes will generate success. The systematic reductions in crime observed are limited (Loesel 2007), depending on a number of factors and dynamics which are beyond the reach of measurable empirical research.

In its extreme form, the evidence-based illusion looks like a kind of charlatanism: it promises what it cannot deliver, while concealing this incapacity in a misty shroud of complicated, magic-like processing.

Being highly scientific must be the ambition of all criminological research, but it will not deliver objective data as a basis for enhancing criminological influence on policy-making.

Embedded criminology

Paul Wiles (2002) and other colleagues see criminology particularly as a scientific expertise on crime and combating crime to inform the authorities' criminal policy. Criminology then would become merged into what Garland (2001) called the "criminality complex". Just as embedded war journalists report within the limits defined by the military and accept military statements as truth, "embedded criminologists" work within the limits defined by mainstream populism and accept the government-defined problems as the real ones.

Mostly, the ambition to evolve towards an 'expertise science' goes together with a claim of strict scientific empiricism. I just evoked the risks of charlatanism linked to such claim. But embedded criminology poses two additional problems.

First, accepting populist visions on crime and punishment keeps a very important aspect of the crime and insecurity problems out of the criminological purview. As argued, the feelings of insecurity and the call for harsher punitiveness rest upon deep social, economic and cultural developments of which capitalist globalization forms the *basso continuo*. These roots of the perception of crime problems are to be investigated by criminological research. Granted, studying these developments is not suitable for traditional positivist research methodology. But one should not limit the field of research for the sake of one single methodology. Such a person would act like the one who lost his watch in the dark, but keeps searching for it under the street lamp, because of the brighter visibility.

Second, embedded criminology feeds a technocratic policy, which is detrimental for democracy. In our more or less democratic regimes, governments do not use social sciences as a whole, but tend to see criminology and other social sciences as a menu. They select – or manipulate through selective financing – the research that fits best into their political options, and then present its results as objective grounds for their policy. Scientific conclusions are selectively presented as irrefutable, suggesting that the governmental options are beyond any doubt; that they cannot but decide as they do. In doing so, governments try to avoid democratic debate, as if their decisions are dictated by "independent grounds for judgment" (Barber 2003: 120, 129-131).

But democracies are at their best in the absence of independent grounds for judgment. Elections will not decide upon the strength of the ferroconcrete for the viaduct over the Meuse River (in Belgium), or upon the best vaccination against influenza. In totalitarian regimes, only the truth advanced by the dictators or religious leaders is accepted as independent grounds for judgement, so that any public debate is excluded. An equally non-democratic technocracy would emerge if scientific results were used as independent grounds for judgment. It is only where there is room for conflicting views, which are to be resolved "responsibly, reasonably and publicly without the guidance of independent consensual norms" (ibid.: 129), that democracy has any vigour.

However, "[S]ocial scientists and political elites have all too often indulged themselves in this form of hypocrisy" (ibid.: 154). The abuse of social sciences as pseudo-independent grounds infects democracy. Social sciences cannot be independent grounds for judgement, given their intrinsic characteristics, and they should not aim to be, given the pursuit of participatory democracy. Policy is not a technocratic game, but a matter of moral and political and ideological preferences, which, in a democratic regime, must be submitted, not to scientists, but to citizens.

Embedded criminology empties the realm for democratic debate on how society can and should cope with the existential anxiety and its multilevel causes. Instead of feeding the democratic debate, it keeps the public uninformed and contributes to insatiable punitive populism, and to a general consumerist attitude in the population, accelerating the negative spiral in the quality of democracy. It is at risk of playing an active role in the hardening of social life, drifting away from solidarity and social justice, and excluding increasingly more subpopulations. Such criminology would end up being a technical science of social exclusion.

About players and floaters

Criminology has to face its social responsibility, which consists of more than producing "objective facts" or supporting "evidence-based policy". Criminology "… can see itself as a kind of specialist underlabourer, a technical specialist… Or it can embrace the world in which crime so loudly resonates and engage the discussion at this level too" (Garland & Sparks 2000b: 18). The choices are typified by Sparks (1997) as "floaters" versus "players". Players try to play as 'useful' actors in the criminological field, to find solutions for the problems defined by the mainstream public and the governments. Floaters try to float over the field and to observe the broader panorama, including the problem definitions themselves.

As just described, current developments in criminology seem to be dominated by the playing orientation. "The decay of critical criminology in the seventies seems to have dried up its intellectual pretensions" (Boutellier 2005: 203, my translation – LW). There is a tendency to see usefulness through the eyes of the consumerist public and the electorally interested governments, and to limit criminological activities within the contours defined by authorities, the public and the media. Such an approach is attractive, because it leads to the rewarding experience of having some influence on policy, and because it is easier to find funding for research. It is respectable, because of its often admirable methodological discipline, leading to provisional beacons of knowledge. Criminological research must also yield technical reports that are mainly relevant to colleagues, practitioners and policy-makers. But its reach is limited, and it is not the only scientific approach desirable.

Such embedded (or "domesticated") criminology lacks wider theoretical reflection and ethical awareness. That is why, in my view, criminology must do more. It must, indeed, 'float' as well. A socially responsible criminology includes questions regarding the definitions of crime, the social economic and cultural roots of criminality and unsafety feelings, and the fundamental options in crime control.

Socially responsible criminology uses its expertise not only to inform govern-ments, but also to address the public, so as to contribute to a more informed public debate on crime and security issues. There is a great need for an "assertive public criminology" (Currie 2007), to add scientific results and questions to the public discourse on crime and crime policy. While "academic criminology may appear … to be a weak competitor with corporate interests, the vengeful, punitive tabloid press and populist politicians … we should recognize that criminological ideas and broader social science theories … have contributed to the discourses through which debate is conducted, problems conceptualized and solutions proposed" (Stenson & Edwards 2001: 69). It is clear that many opinions on crime and crime control that are now common but not always commonly accepted are deeply rooted in criminological research, such as, for example the inaccuracy of recorded crime as an estimate of real crime; poverty and social exclusion as a breeding ground for criminality; the disastrous impact of negative prejudices and stigmatisation on crime and crime control; the poor efficiency of the punitive apriorism in responding to crime; the need for social policy in radical crime prevention; the potential of restorative justice.

Besides informing authorities on the conditions in which they can take their decisions, social sciences must first of all inform the public on the conditions, the possible options and their eventual consequences, so that the options and decisions are based on the best possible information. It is the difference between populist decision-making, based on a narrow view of short-term benefits with a lack of information on the broader context and longer-term consequences, on the one hand, and the truly participatory democratic decision-making, based on an informed public debate with a view on an overall picture of the conditions and longer prospects, on the other. Note that I did not write 'the' overall picture, because social sciences can offer only 'an' overall picture. But at least an overall picture, and often even several different overall pictures, based on different scientific approaches.

A risk is, however, that "floating criminology" would deteriorate into "evangelical criminology" (Pratt 2006), a movement rather than a science, grounded on "taken-for-granted status that can blind its followers... to its problems and dilemma's" (ibid.: 45/47). Pratt refers in his article especially to the evangelical zeal in promoting restorative justice; we could add to it some tendencies in prevention, treatment of delinquency and also a few very wide macro-theoretical constructions which lack critical scientific grounds or sound empirical support. But still, such wide studies must be made, because they are fundamental to understand the current penal populism. And accepting the current penal populism as "taken-for-granted" certainly is unscientific.

Between evangelism and charlatanism

I am not presenting a simple opposition between the good floater and the ugly player. Both are necessary, and both may go wrong. Floaters may choose an easy life, staying on the sideline and keeping their hands clean. In the worst case, they become unworldly, irrelevant constructivists or sceptical negativists, condemning all attempts to act as insufficient, wrongly conceived, serving a hidden agenda, co-opted by authoritarian forces, or produced by simpletons.

In the best case, they offer thoughtful analyses, broad visions or motivating utopian views which offer significant intellectual references for those who act in the real world, the players who make necessary compromises to realize changes.

Players get their hands dirty, but they can play dirty as well. Some indeed act as cynical careerists, seeking the money wherever embedded research can be done, without any concern for its potential counterproductive effects on a considerable part of the population. Other players, however, try to conceive and carry out the best possible experiments resulting from well thought-out compromises between ideals designed while floating and reality observed while playing. In my view, the need is for a balanced scientific criminology, which combines both floating and playing, and delivers strong empirical work to avoid criminological evangelism (Pratt 2006), and well thought-out broad social theory to avoid charlatanism.

There is nothing wrong with social ethical reflections to orient social scientific research, on the contrary. However, such reflection must be flanked by good and systematically constructed theorizing and critically guided by high level empirical research. While it is important to distinguish clearly what we found from what we think and what we hope, social scientists also must think and hope.

By way of conclusion

Criminology is not a laboratory science. It operates in the delicate field where people and societal institutions confront each other; people victimise other people; citizens' rights and liberties are at stake; families are torn apart, and some people are even brought to death. All this is carried out with the use of power, which carries the risk of abuse of power. Recent developments increasingly position democracy at odds with its own principles: in view of 'preserving democratic liberties', liberties are cut. The populist obsession with crime, justice and (un)safety entails an increasing appeal to criminological expertise. But in a world dominated by a ruthless struggle for individualistic power and wealth, criminology cannot just sit aside and count the strokes. Even the option to work within the official chalk marks and 'to stay away from politics' is an ideological and political choice: to accept the problems as they are defined by the powerful and to contribute to their more efficient functioning.

By doing good and not embedded scientific research in the field of crime, unsafety and justice and its wide contextual conditions, and by addressing its findings also to the public forum, criminology can take on its active responsibility in the pursuit of a more just, more solidarity driven, and more participatory democracy.

References

Barber, B. (2003), *Strong Democracy. Participatory politics for a new age*, Berkeley: Univ. California Press, 20th anniversary edition.

Bauman, Z. (2000), Social Uses of Law and Order. In D. Garland and R. Sparks (eds.), *Criminology and Social Theory*, Oxford: Oxford University Press, 23-46.

Baumann, Z. (2000b), *Liquid Modernity*, Cambridge: Polity Press.

Baumann, Z. (2004), *Wasted Lives. Modernity and its Outcasts*, Cambridge: Polity Press.

Beck, U. (1992), *Risk Society*, London: Sage.

Boutellier, H. (1996), Beyond the criminal justice paradox. Alternatives between law and morality. *European Journal of Criminal Policy and Research* (4), 4 : 7-20.

Boutellier, H. (2005), *De Veiligheidsutopie. Hedendaags Onbehagen en Verlangen rond Misdaad en Straf*, Den Haag: Boom Juridische Uitgevers, 3e druk.

Buruma, Y. (2005), *De Dreigingsspiraal. Onbedoelde Neveneffecten van Misdaadbestrijding*, Den Haag: Boom Juridische Uitgevers.

Castel, R. (2003), *L'insécurité Sociale. Qu'est-ce qu'être protégé* ? Paris: Ed. du Seuil.

Chancer, L. & E. McLaughlin (2007), Public criminologies. Diverse perspectives on academia and policy. *Theoretical Criminology* (11), 2: 155-173.

Currie, E. (2007), Against marginality. Arguments for a public criminology. *Theoretical Criminology* (11), 2 : 175-190.

Daems, T. (2007), *Making Sense of Penal Change: Punishment, Victimization & Society*, Ph.D. Thesis in Criminology, Leuven: K.U.Leuven, Faculty of Law; published as: Daems, T. (2008), *Making Sense of Penal Change,* Oxford: Oxford University Press.

Farrington, D. (1991), The English criminological utopia has arrived. In J. Junger-Tas & I. Sagel-Grande (eds.), *Criminology in the 21st Century*, Leuven: Garant.

Garland, D. & R. Sparks (2000), Criminology, social theory and the challenge of our times. In D. Garland & R. Sparks (eds.) (2000), *Criminology and Social Theory*, Oxford: Oxford University Press, Clarendon Studies in Criminology, 1-22.

Garland, D. & R. Sparks (eds.) (2000), *Criminology and Social Theory*, Oxford: Oxford University Press, Clarendon Studies in Criminology.

Garland, D. (1996), The limits of the sovereign state: strategies of crime control in contemporary society. *British Journal of Criminology* (36) : 445-471.

Garland, D. (2001), *The Culture of Control. Crime and Social Order in Contemporary Society*, Oxford: Oxford University Press.

Giddens, A. (1998), Risk society: the context of British politics. In J. Franklin (ed.), *The politics of Risk Society*, Cambridge: Polity.

Goris, P. (2001), Community crime prevention and the 'partnership approach': a safe community for all? *European Journal on Criminal Policy and Research* (9), 4: 447-457.

Haggerty, K. (2004), Displaced expertise: Three constraints on the policy-relevance of criminological thought. *Theoretical Criminology* (8), 2: 211-232.

Hebberecht, P. & F. Sack (eds.) (1997), *La prévention de la délinquance en Europe: nouvelles stratégies*, Paris : L'Harmattan.

Kappeler, V., M. Blumberg & G. Potter (eds.) (2000), *The Mythology of Crime and Criminal Justice*, Prospect Heights (Ill.): Waveland Press, 3th.

Karstedt, S. & K. Bussmann (eds.) (2000), *Social Dynamics of Crime and Control. New Theories for a World in Transition*, Oxford: Hart Publishing.

Karstedt, S. & S. Farrall (2004), The Moral Maze of the Middle Class. The Predatory Society and its Emerging Regulatory Order. In H. Albrecht, T. Serassis, & H. Kania, (eds.), *Images of Crime II*. Freiburg i. Br.: Ed. Iuscrim, 65 – 94.

Karstedt, S. & S. Farrall (2007*), Law Abiding Majority? The everyday crimes of the middle classes*. Briefing 3, July 2007, London: Centre for Crime and Justice Studies.

Kutchinsky, B. (1979), Law, crime and legal attitudes: new advances in Scandinavian research on knowledge and opinion about law. In S. Mednick & S. Shoham (eds.), *New Paths in Criminology*, Lexington (Mass.): Heath & Co, 191-218.

Lianos, M. & M. Douglas (2000), Dangerization and the end of deviance. In D. Garland & R. Sparks (eds.), *Criminology and Social Theory*, Oxford: Oxford University Press, Clarendon Studies in Criminology, 103-125.

Loesel, F. (2007), It's never too early and never too late: towards an integrated science of developmental intervention in criminology. *The Criminologist* (32), 5: 1-8.

Merton, R. (1938), Social structure and anomie. *American Sociological Review* (3):672-682.

Messner, S. & R Rosenfeld (1994), *Crime and the American Dream*, Belmont (CA): Wadsworth Publishing.

O'Malley, P. (2006), Risk and restorative justice: governing through the minimization of harms. In I. Aertsen, T. Daems & L. Robert (eds.), *Institutionalizing Restorative Justice*, Cullompton (UK): Willan Publishing, 216-236.

Pratt, J. (2006), Beyond evangelical criminology: in meaning and significance of restorative justice. In I. Aertsen, T. Daems & L. Robert (eds.), *Institutionalizing Restorative Justice*, Cullompton (UK), Willan Publishing, 44-67.

Putnam, R. (2000), *Bowling Alone*, New York: Simon and Schuster.

Roberts, J., L. Stalans, D. Indermaur & M. Hough (2003), *Penal Populism and Public Opinion. Lessons form Five Countries*, Oxford: Oxford University Press.

Sherman, L. (2005), The use and usefulness of criminology, 1751-2005: enlightenment of justice and its failures. *Annals AAPS* 600: 115-135.

Sparks, R. (1997), Recent social theory and the study of crime and punishment. In *The Oxford Handbook of Criminology*, Oxford: Oxford Univ. Press, 2nd edition, 409-435.

Stenson, K. & A. Edwards (2001), Rethinking crime control in advanced liberal government: the 'third way' and the return to the local. In K. Stenson & R. Sullivan (eds.), *Crime, Risk and Justice. The Politics of Crime Control in Liberal Democracies*, Cullompton (UK): Willan Publishing, 68-86.

Stenson, K. & R. Sullivan (eds.) (2001), *Crime, Risk and Justice. The Politics of Crime Control in Liberal Democracies*, Cullompton (UK): Willan Publishing.

Stenson, K. (2001), The new politics of crime control. In K. Stenson & R. Sullivan (eds.), *Crime, Risk and Justice. The Politics of Crime Control in Liberal Democracies*, Cullompton (UK): Willan Publishing, 15-28.

Taylor, J., P. Walton & J. Young (1973), *The New Criminology*, London: Routledge.

Tittle, Ch. (1995), *Control Balance. Toward a general theory of deviance*, Boulder (Co.): Westview Press.

Wacquant, L. (1999), *Les Prisons de la Misère*, Paris: Liber, Raison d'agir.

Walgrave, L. (2008), *Restorative Justice, Self-Interest and Responsible Citizenship*, Cullompton (UK): Willan Publishing.

Wiles, P. (2002), Criminology in the twenty-first century: public good or private interest? *Australian and New Zealand Journal of Criminology* (35): 238-252.

Wood, J. & B. Dupont (2006) (eds.), *Democracy, Society and the Governance of Security*, Cambridge: Cambridge University Press.

Young, J. (1999), *The Exclusive Society*, London: Sage.

Zedner, L. (2003), Too much security? *International Journal of the Sociology of Law* (31): 155-184.

OUR SENSE OF JUSTICE: VALUES, JUSTICE AND PUNISHMENT

Susanne Karstedt

Introduction: Meeting a Republican

As much as the criminological community has endorsed John Braithwaite's theory of shaming, and the idea, concept and practice of restorative justice, as little attention criminologists have paid to the conceptual framework where he situated these ideas. *A Republican Theory of Criminal Justice* – the subtitle to *Not Just Deserts* which was written in collaboration with political philosopher Philip Pettit (1990) - was published shortly after the path breaking *Crime, Shame and Reintegration* (1989), and in his collection of essays Braithwaite (2002: 12) reiterated and strengthened the link between restorative justice and a republican perspective. He named the following dimensions of restorative justice as important from a "republican perspective": "restoring property loss, restoring injury, restoring a sense of security, restoring dignity, restoring a sense of empowerment, restoring deliberative democracy, restoring harmony based on a feeling that justice has been done, and restoring social support." In *Not Just Deserts* he broadened the republican perspective and transcended the field of restorative justice. He called for a "Republican Criminology" to address the problem of inequality as one of genuine concern for criminologists (1995a), and embedded the emerging theory of regulation and criminal justice ("Speaking softly and carrying sticks") in a republican perspective on the separation of powers (1997).

Republican theory and republicanism are of twofold importance for Braithwaite's work, as he wrote in 2000 (Braithwaite 2000). Republicanism provides "an explanatory as well as a normative connection" for restorative justice. Braithwaite here follows the tradition of giving normative grounding to criminal justice, and in linking both empirical and normative theory he does not deviate from other routes of establishing the foundations for criminal justice like deterrence theory. It is by no ways a coincidence that he develops his republican perspective by contesting deterrence theory which can be deemed the only rival theory of criminal justice that encompasses both an empirical and normative dimension (Braithwaite and Pettit 1990). Republicanism defines the values on which restorative justice rests and the objectives it should achieve as "restoring" the lives of individuals and communities (1995b), and sets the objectives for criminal justice more broadly. "Republican Criminological Praxis" would shift the focus from street crime to corporate crime, and would endorse a top-down transfer of criminal procedures by handing restorative practices from which mainly elite offenders have profited so far, down to street crime offenders, and channelling the more severe sanctions traditionally meted out to street crime offenders up to elite criminals (1995c).

Surprisingly, the republican perspective of restorative justice includes a democratic dimension, namely "restoring deliberative democracy". In fact, Braithwaite's republicanism has a strong democratic strand. The Tocquevillean vision of democratic communities perpetually deliberating and reassuring themselves of their common values and morality is part and parcel of Braithwaite's republicanism, and finds its expression in the very idea of restorative justice and its communicative and deliberative elements. Further to this, Braithwaite's republicanism has a strong foundation in egalitarian values and attitudes. In contrast to republican perspectives that endorse a more meritocratic egalitarianism as e.g. in the US or the UK, Braithwaite's republicanism supports welfare policies and an egalitarianism that does not neglect those who ultimately failed and struggled (see below). His republicanism reminds me of a (true?) story about the people from my hometown Lübeck, one of the oldest and longest lasting republics of Europe, told by Thomas Mann in his Nobel prize winning novel *Buddenbrooks. The Decline of a Family.*

As the revolution of 1848 finally reached Lübeck, a crowd gathered in front of the house of the mayor, who was then head of a sovereign state. When he asked them in Low German dialect what they wanted, the answer was "We want a republic!" and the following exchange ensued: "You have already got one!" - "Then give us another one". What exactly is the merit of republicanism and republican theory, if democracies which admittedly would profit from improvements, and democratic theory were already in place?

In this contribution I wish to explore Braithwaite's republican theory and confront it with results from two cross-cultural studies. I analyse the impact of value patterns on two decisive and significant features of criminal justice: the use of (illegal) violence by the state, mainly in criminal justice –, and punishment. i.e. the numbers of individuals who are deprived of liberty and the ways in which this is done. Taken together the two studies will help to understand the role of values in criminal justice generally, and the normative thrust of republican values in particular.

Normative theory and the question of values

Braithwaite unambiguously has brought values back into criminological reasoning. Values had been admitted to criminological discourse only as subjects of critique and de-constructing efforts. The denunciation of values as deeply flawed was based on conceptualising them as ideological dimensions of a "superstructure" that shaped criminal justice systems and accounted for its worst features. From the rational choice and liberal point of view, values are superseded by rational decision making, and deterrence is the predominant mechanism through which social order and norm compliance can be achieved by the criminal justice system. Braithwaite did not subscribe to either of these positions, and in a most courageous move outlined and constructed a normative theory, certainly a no-go area for many criminologists. He argued that the criminological knowledge base could provide the foundations for a normative theory of justice, and given its empirical foundations a normative theory would have measurable results in terms of more justice and less crime when put into practice (Braithwaite and Pettit 2000). Any conception of criminal justice (and regulation) should be based on more than one mechanism of compliance, as individuals were not only rational beings, but also moral beings striving to live up to their own values and those of their community (see Braithwaite and Drahos 2000).

A normative theory should provide answers to the key normative questions of criminal justice that criminologists have found difficult. What types of behaviour should be deterred, shamed and prohibited, how should justice be done, and what sanctions should be provided? As criminological theories are mostly mute on these questions, republican theory informed by philosophical and political reasoning indeed is in a position to provide answers to these questions. Its key elements as developed by Braithwaite and Pettit (1990, 2000) are based on two foundational values: autonomy and freedom of the individual, defined as non-domination by others and freedom from interference, and equality as a necessary precondition for the equal enjoyment of autonomy and freedom.

Republicanism thus transcends the mere notion of non-interference by individuals, governments, and states, and instead "require(s) the *assurance* of not being exposed to the possibility of arbitrary interference by an uncontrolled power " (Braithwaite 2000: 89; emphasis added). As such assurance can best be achieved through active participation of and deliberation among individuals, delivery of justice that strives for this ideal should be participatory and deliberative, all the more as criminal justice implies without any doubt acts of domination and interference into the liberty of individuals. Restorative justice is capable of providing these participatory and deliberative forms of justice in practice. Normative republican theory of justice therefore is not a mere utopian vision, which lacks the connection with practice. Braithwaite's scholarship indeed integrates "concrete and normative aspects" in a way aptly described by Koskenniemi (2005, 20): "By lacking connection with practice [scholarship] ... would seem unable to demonstrate its norms in a tangible fashion. It would seem utopian. If [the normative aspect] was lacking then scholarship would lack critical distance from state behaviour, will or interest."

A normative theory of justice therefore implies that its norms and the values on which it rests have an empirical foundation and are part of the practice to which they refer. Values of justice are experienced and lived in communities, as Herbert Mead noted in 1918: "We do not respect law in the abstract but the values which the laws of the community preserve" (Mead 1964, 220). Laws should provide a vision of justice, as they need to rule the imagination of individuals and collectives before they can govern the state. The republican principle of freedom from arbitrary interference by the powerful particularly defines the realm of (international) human rights, where morality, values and policy are inextricably linked. Consequently Donnelly's observation on human rights equally applies to Braithwaite's republican theory of justice, that "... built into ...their very character is ... an interaction between moral vision and political reality" (Donnelly, 1985, 32).

This provides us with the key to an empirical test of republican theory as a normative theory of justice. Values of freedom from interference and equality need to direct the actions of communities, institutions and individuals, and where they dominate more, not less and better justice should be found. Our sense of justice and the values on which it is based guide the forms of justice that we find acceptable or unacceptable. Both define the ways in which we allow criminal justice and particularly punishment to interfere with the freedom of individuals, and non-egalitarian hierarchies to be established through criminal punishment. They thus guide the form of justice we want to achieve and define the objectives of justice that we seek, and as such values are open for empirical analysis.

The first of the two republican values is explicitly linked to republican and liberal traditions, while egalitarian values have their roots more in democratic rather than republican traditions. As Michael Mann (2005) observes, the strong emphasis on egalitarian values endangers democracies as this fosters a drive towards interference with liberties. Braithwaite is aware of the tensions and potential imbalances between the two basic values in his republican theory; he therefore insists on strong egalitarian values that are capable of counteracting the forces of liberal non-interference, or even might overrule non-interference in some instances. Assurance of non-interference can only be guaranteed if powers are separated, calibrated and attenuated (Braithwaite 1997), and egalitarian values are the seedbed of the institutions that can deliver such assurance for individuals and communities. While republicans and democrats share these values, they assign a different weight and importance to them.

A study of values and punishment

Non-interference, equality and punishment

We expect that in republican or democratic communities criminal punishment expresses or at least relates to the values that these communities hold. Intuitively, values should shape the regimes of criminal punishment that communities adopt and that are supported by their populations. Both values are vital in shaping the regimes and institutions of punishment (see e.g. Whitman 2003). Values of individual autonomy, freedom and non-interference should clearly restrict the power of criminal justice institutions, support due process and also reduce restrictions of freedom that are imposed as sanctions. Further, these values should impact on the treatment of offenders within the criminal justice system, which implies treating them with dignity and the respect that individuals can expect from and are afforded by democratic and republican institutions alike, by those who represent these as well as their fellow citizens. Values of autonomy should reduce interference with individual liberty to the necessary minimum. Egalitarian values are important as they define the status that we are willing to afford to offenders, and the ways in which we are inclined to treat them as one of us. Egalitarian values define practices and politics of status. They restrict power and the powerful, as well as the exertion of power by those invested with it. They delineate the extent to which status differences shape everyday encounters, and the extent to which any kind of debasing or degrading treatment is accepted as an expression of status differences. Criminal punishment therefore signifies and redefines status differences (Whitman 2003).

Countries where values of individual autonomy and individual freedom are dominant, as well as countries with high levels of egalitarian values will differ in their regimes of punishment from those with less emphasis on individual autonomy and higher levels of authoritarian or non-egalitarian values; the latter generally having higher imprisonment rates and harsher punishment regimes. However, the two values are unfolding in two distinct patterns. Where non-interference is dominating, egalitarianism is meritocratic, which represents the republican-liberal tradition. Where non-interference is given less weight, egalitarianism is defined by substantive equality, a pattern that represents democratic and welfare states. These different patterns should be discernible even in societies with mature and stable democratic institutions and governments and should account for differences in imprisonment rates and prison conditions. Finally, the precarious nature of both values becomes visible when structural inequality is high, and the reality of living conditions and the distribution of chances widely differ from egalitarian ideals and values (Braithwaite 1995a). Such tensions between values and structure should make criminal justice harsher, both in terms of imprisonment rates and prison conditions.

Republicanism would prefer *chance-oriented or absolute meritocratic* egalitarianism, whilst democracies would prefer strong or *outcome-oriented* egalitarianism. Chance-oriented egalitarianism assumes that individuals have equal chances, but concedes that individuals make bad choices and do not use the chances open to them. Outcome-oriented egalitarianism in contrast focuses on amending where social injustice disadvantages people thoroughly. Chance-oriented meritocratic egalitarianism is characterised by low interference, whilst outcome-oriented egalitarianism implies a higher level of interference. Chance oriented meritocratic egalitarianism not only allows for considerable status differences, but also defines them as functioning as incentives for integration and compliance. This type of value pattern and the ensuing status practices are epitomised by the steep 'fall from grace' in case of failure, and exclusion in the case of non-compliance. Need is seen as the result of personal failure, rather than social injustice. In contrast, outcome-oriented egalitarianism focuses on reducing status differences, and on achieving inclusion by supporting even those who fail. It thus attenuates the absolute meritocratic position. The United States represent chance-oriented egalitarianism, while e.g. Scandinavian and other European countries like Germany represent outcome-oriented egalitarianism.

Where value patterns are dominated by chance-oriented egalitarianism, penal regimes should operate in a way that increases status differences between offenders and others; confirming and deepening status differences are both built into the practices of punishment regimes, resulting in harsher sentencing practices and penal regimes than in countries with outcome-oriented egalitarianism. Three hypotheses will be explored:

(a) values of individual autonomy and non-interference as well as egalitarian values generally reduce the harshness of criminal justice;
(b) the specific patterns of egalitarianism account for differences between punishment regimes in mature democracies;
(c) tensions between democratic values and actual status differences and equality account for differences between punishment regimes in mature democracies.

Data

The analyses are based on a cross-national sample of 67 countries, for which data on penal regimes, value patterns and structural indicators were collected. The data are spanning a period from the 1980s for the first wave of the World Value Survey until 2005. The data on penal regimes are covering the period from 1999-2005, and mean values for the respective periods are used. Two indicators of the penal regime are used, the rate of imprisonment and prison conditions. The rate of imprisonment was based on Walmsley's data base (Walmsley 1999-2009). The rating of prison conditions was based on the Country Reports from the US State Department (1999-2006) and Neapolitano's (2001) ratings, which were extended from three to five ranks. These indicate that (1) prisons 'meet minimum standards', (2) 'meet minimum standards with some deficits', usually caused by overcrowding, (3) 'do not meet minimum standards', (4) have 'harsh but not life threatening conditions', and (5) are 'life threatening'. Both indicators are not correlated, and prison conditions (which do not include the U.S.) are only linked to the average length of prison sentences.

Measurement of the values of individual autonomy and egalitarianism are based on a study by Hofstede (Hofstede & Hofstede 2005), and are presently available for more than 60 countries. These value patterns are related to cultural and social practices, and as such represent 'lived values' rather than ideals. 'Individualism/ Collectivism' measures the detachment from traditional group and family bonds, and as such non-interference and freedom from domination by others, particularly groups. This pattern emphasises individual autonomy and achievement, and thus meritocratic and individualistic values. As such it represents the first and most republican of the two values. 'Power Distance' in Hofstede's original terminology, or 'Egalitarianism' defines the extent to which relationships of dominance, power and subordination, and hierarchical relationships between different social groups prevail or are replaced by more egalitarian orientations. As such it represents the egalitarian component of the republican and democratic value pattern. High values on the 'Individualism' scale indicate strong individualism, and high values on the 'Egalitarianism' scale indicate egalitarian value patterns. In all Western industrialized societies, including Australia and New Zealand, high Individualism is the dominating value pattern, while in Latin American and Islamic countries mostly collectivistic orientations prevail. Asian societies have a medium to strong collectivistic orientation. Western industrialized countries, with the exception of Latin European countries (e.g. France and Italy), rank at the higher end of the egalitarianism scale, while Latin American and Asian countries are characterized by a comparably low level of egalitarian values. Both value patterns are strongly correlated to the Polity Index (Marshall & Jaggers 2005) and the Freedom House Index of Civil Liberties, indicating that they foster those institutions that ensure freedom of non-interference as well as egalitarianism (see Triandis and Trafimov 2001; Jaggers and Gurr 1995).

The variables indicating chance-oriented/ meritocratic or outcome-oriented egalitarianism were selected from the four waves of the World Value Survey from 1982, 1990, 1995 and 2000. They are measured as the mean percentage of those who supported the following statements in all waves available in a country, with high levels of support indicating the chance-oriented / meritocratic value pattern and low levels pointing towards outcome-oriented egalitarianism: 'We need larger income differences as incentives'; and 'Laziness or lack of willpower' as 'reason why people live in need in this country'. Two indicators of structural inequality were used, the Gini-Index of income inequality (United Nations 2002), and the index of ethnic fractionalisation, which measures the level of differentiation between ethnic groups in a country (Alesina *et al.* 2003).

Analyses comprise of two steps: first, penal regimes are compared for different levels of individualistic and egalitarian value patterns; second, differences in values and status practices are analysed for mature democracies. The definition of mature democracies is based on the Polity Index (Marshall and Jaggers 2005), which ranks countries on a scale from 'autocratic' (- 10) to 'fully democratic' (+ 10), with 'mature democracies' ranking between +8 and +10. In this way, a more homogeneous sample was achieved, in which the institutional assurance of non-interference was at similar, high and sufficient levels, and thus, the actual contribution of values could be more precisely assessed.

Results

Both individualistic and egalitarian values have an impact on prison conditions in the sample that comprises of all 67 countries, as figures 1a, b and 2a, b show. The more individual autonomy is valued, and the more egalitarian values are adopted, the better are prison conditions. However, countries with higher levels of individualistic values do not significantly differ or even have slightly higher imprisonment rates than collectivistic countries.[1] The exceptional position of the United States is clearly visible in this pattern (Figure 1b and 2b). Individualism as it generates respect for individual autonomy and enhances reluctance in interfering with liberties of others, and egalitarianism, as it reduces power differentials and attenuates degrading status strategies, both impact on the ways in which offenders are punished, however they do not affect the use of imprisonment in criminal justice systems. The cultural and institutional practices that build on these values shape criminal justice. Countries ranking high on these values might not punish less, but they treat those in prison better. This holds true for mature democracies; with a certain level of institutional assurance of non-interference given, both values show the same pattern of impact, a significant impact in the case of prison conditions, and none for imprisonment rates. This speaks to a rather robust impact of values on punishment regimes (not shown).

Penal regimes further differ between countries with chance-oriented merito-cratic value patterns and those with outcome-oriented egalitarianism, even if comparable levels of institutional assurance of non-interference are given in mature democracies (Figure 3 and 4). Both indicators of chance-oriented meritocratic egalitarianism point towards a significant impact on prison conditions, however are not linked to rates of imprisonment. If the population of a country support large income differences, and deem laziness a reason

---

[1] This applies with and without inclusion of the U.S.

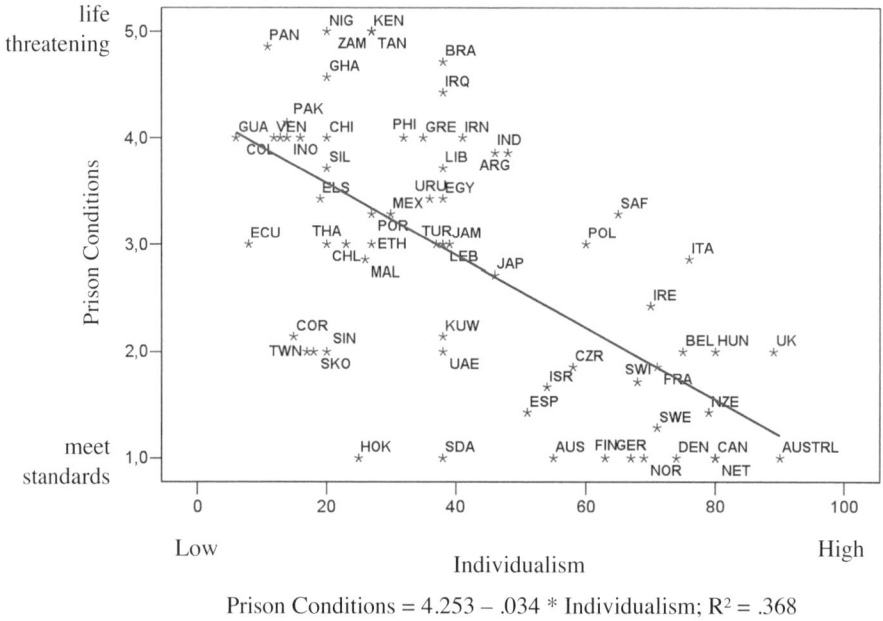

Prison Conditions = 4.253 – .034 * Individualism; R² = .368

Figure 1a: Individualism and Prison Conditions 1999-2005

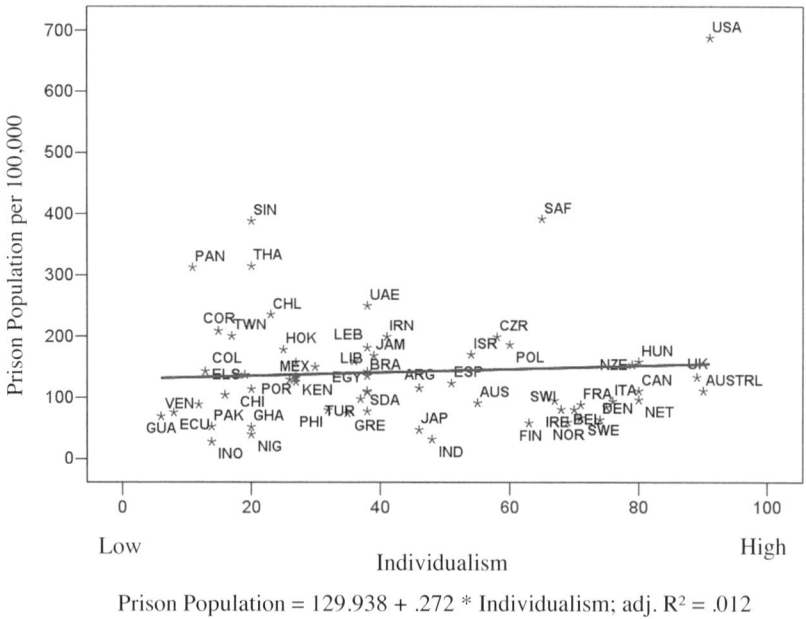

Prison Population = 129.938 + .272 * Individualism; adj. R² = .012

Figure 1b: Individualism and Prison Population (per 100,000) 1999-2005

Prison Conditions = 4.483 - .036 * Egalitarianism; R² = .360

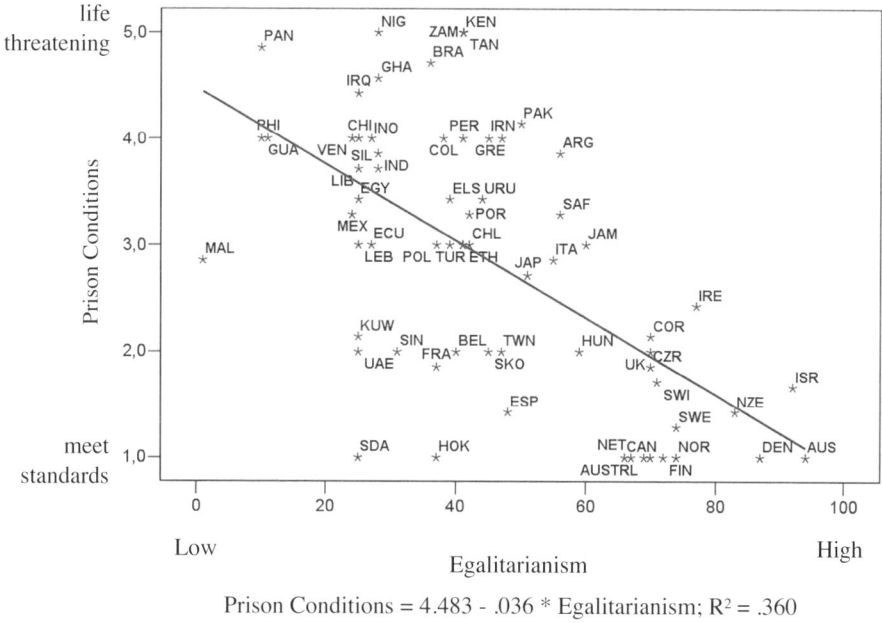

Figure 2a: Egalitarianism and Prison Conditions 1999-2005

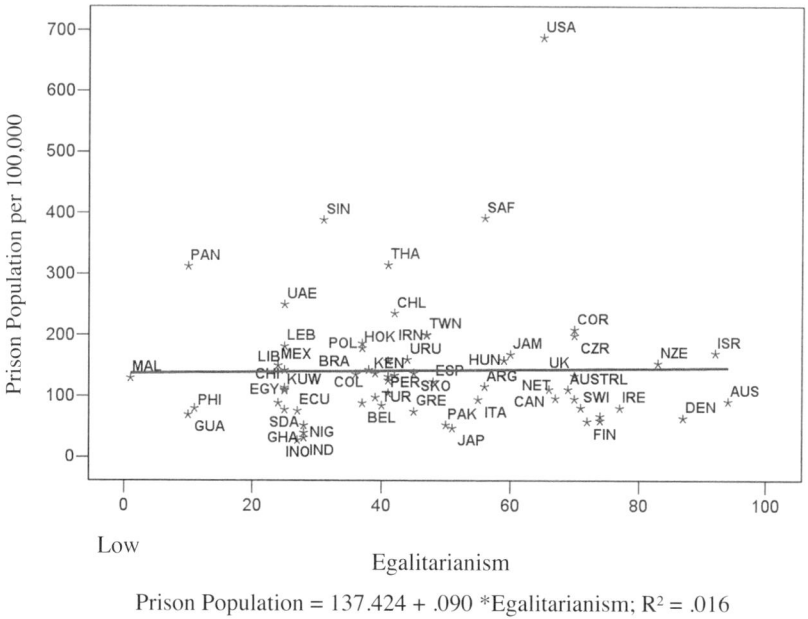

Prison Population = 137.424 + .090 *Egalitarianism; R² = .016

Figure 2b: Egalitarianism and Prison Population (per 100,000) 1999-2005

of need, offenders in prison live under worse conditions than in countries where the population is more in favour of the opposing statements. The chance-oriented meritocratic pattern distinctly and significantly coincides with deteriorating prison conditions. In addition, where laziness is seen as a cause of poverty, rates of imprisonment increase significantly (United States included).[2] Republican egalitarianism with a strong emphasis on non-interference makes punishment regimes harsher, as it fosters attitudes that support debasing and degrading status practices in dealing with offenders, of which harsh prison conditions are just one expression.

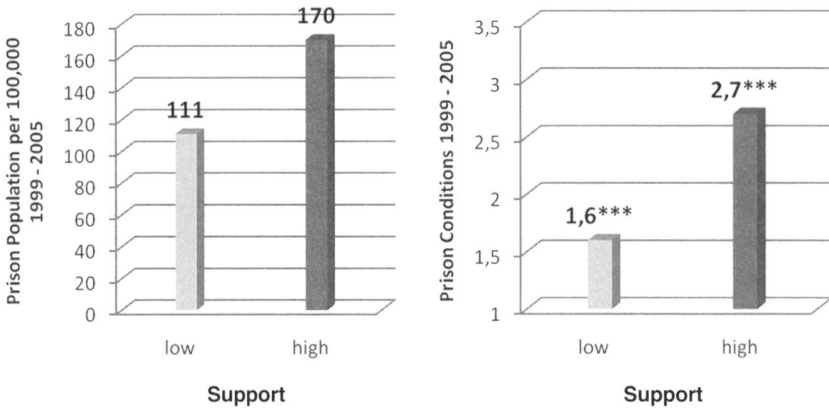

Figure 3: Mature Democracies: Support for Large Income Differences, Prison Population and Prison Conditions 1999- 2005

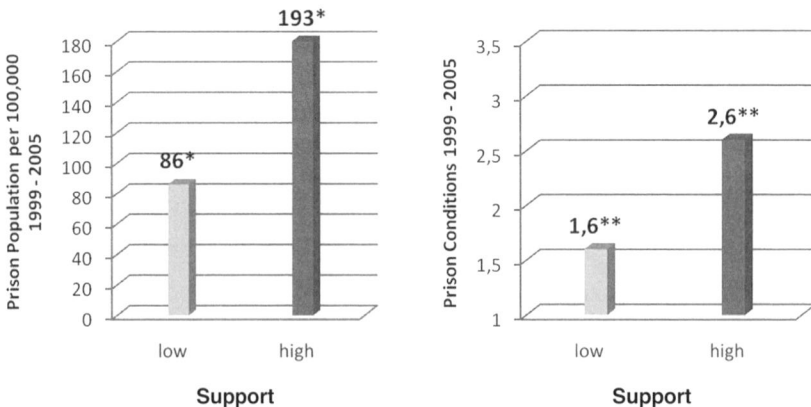

Figure 4: Mature Democracies: Support for Laziness as Reason for Personal Need, Prison Population and Prison Conditions 1999- 2005

---

2   The results do not differ if the U.S. are excluded.

Actual structural inequality and ethnic fractionalisation both have an impact on prison conditions and imprisonment rates in mature democracies (Figure 5 and 6). Structural inequality significantly increases the rate of imprisonment, and both considerably and significantly downgrade prison conditions. Whether such structural inequalities are supported by the specific meritocratic value pattern, or in themselves challenge the foundational values and thus produce additional tensions in societies that perceive of themselves as egalitarian, cannot be decided (see Karstedt 2006). However, the results show that republican values need a strong foundation in social equality and inclusion if they are to improve criminal justice, as Braithwaite (1995a) so convincingly argued.

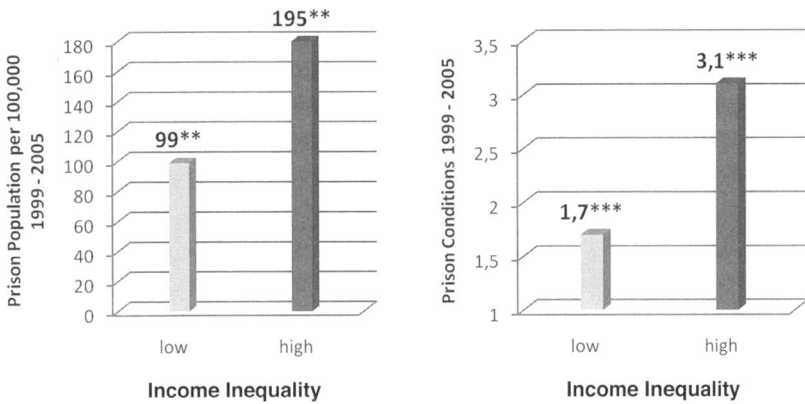

Figure 5: Mature Democracies: Income Inequality, Prison Population and Prison Conditions 1999- 2005

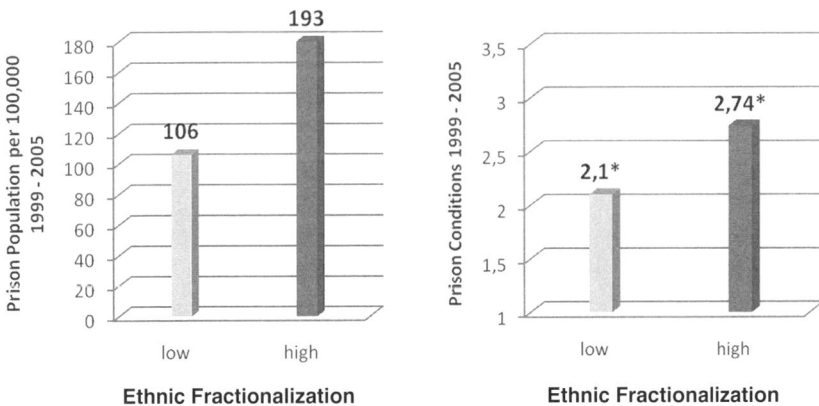

Figure 6: Mature Democracies: Ethnic Fractionalization, Prison Population and Prison Conditions 1999- 2005

A study of values and state violence

The egalitarian foundations of non-interference and state violence

State violence exemplifies the 'arbitrary interference by an uncontrolled power' from which republican values and institutions should protect citizens; it violates if not the laws of the country itself then the human rights of its citizens. This poses a dilemma, as the (nation) state is responsible for guaranteeing and assuring non-interference and the respective rights of citizens in the first instance. The legacy of early republican theory was (and still is) a lasting paradox. It introduced the notion of individual autonomy and liberty, and thus of freedom from unlawful interference and deprivation, and simultaneously invested the state with the task to secure these rights and act as their guarantor, including its very own actions. The state is thus 'both the guardian of basic rights and ... the behemoth against which one's rights need to be defended' (Ishay 2004: 363). Freedom from unlawful interference by the state, it seems therefore requires a reasonably strong state, that is capable of monitoring its own institutions, agents and representatives that they do not transgress the boundaries of minimal and necessary interference and comply with the respective norms of conduct.

Consequently in failed states or transitional countries, violence by the state prevails and reaches extraordinarily high levels. As Juan Mendez and his colleagues (1999) describe, this gives rise to high levels of 'lawless violence' in Latin America, predominantly in criminal justice institutions (see Caldeira and Hollstein 1999). According to Mendez, lawless violence indicates a "clear abdication of democratic authority (of the state)" (Mendez 1999: 19). The state is not capable of restraining its own bodies in providing security and guaranteeing physical integrity to its citizens, nor do governments put a lot of effort into restraining state violence. In 2007, in one Brazilian state alone, more than 2,000 people were killed by police, most of whom were very young and many of them living on the streets. The lack of physical security for its citizens is a defining characteristic of the failing state, and their governments are deeply implicated themselves; my own data show that the Failed States Index (Fund for Peace 2005 – 2009) as well as its individual dimensions like the rise of factionalised elites or delegitimisation of its institutions correlate with the index of state violence, that is used in this study at about r=.80.[3]

From early on, John Braithwaite has emphasised that for republican values to thrive both a strong state and civil society are needed, and he has never been an advocate of a weak state (1998; 2000). Strong states are capable of restricting unlawful use of violence by their agencies, and a strong civil society will monitor such abuse. As necessary as freedom of the press, opposition parties and other principles and institutions of government are, as important are values and moral visions amongst the public. Criminal justice agents are part of these communities, and often engage in unlawful violence in the belief that they are expressing the wish of a silent majority. Citizens need to be willing to stand up for their visions of freedom and non-interference: acting against state violence means "acting as if the rule of law existed and by doing so, challenging others to do so as well" (Goldston 1999: 463). Values embody the moral vision that counts in communities, and guides their sense of justice. "The rule of law must train its citizens to see themselves and their communities one way rather than the other" Kahn 1999, 83). State violence needs to be named, blamed and shamed, but also prosecuted.

State violence is rarely indiscriminate and targets all citizens / inhabitants of a nation state. It is decisive that it is directed against specific groups that are singled out, be they ethnic and religious minorities, elites, professionals, political opposition parties, opponents of the regime, the young and the poor, offenders, or any combination of these. The values of non-interference and egalitarianism are equally fundamental, as freedom from arbitrary and unlawful interference has to be equally distributed, and the relevant principles and procedures have to apply to everybody independent of their affiliation to specific groups. As state violence targets minority positions of all kinds and from all ranks, both moral condemnation of state violence and taking action require a strong sense of egalitarian and non-discriminating values within society. Citizens need to perceive themselves as part of the same 'moral collective' in order to fight state violence against specific and singled-out groups. Mass atrocities often start with severing ties of allegiance between the majority and the targeted group, and excluding the latter from the 'moral

---

[3]   The Failed States Index is published by the Fund for Peace and has been developed as part of an early warning system since 2005, comprising of 177 countries in 2009, which are ranked according to 12 criteria, each on a scale from 0 (low intensity) to 10 (high intensity). The 12 criteria cover an array of demographic, economic and political indicators, see http://www. fundforpeace.org/web/index.php?option=com_content&task=view&id=99&Itemid=323.

universe' of the community and humankind. Structural divisions like income inequality or ethnic fractionalization further restrict the outreach between social groups that seems to be a prerequisite for support of egalitarianism when acting against state violence.

This study explores the impact of both value patterns – autonomy / non-interference and egalitarianism – on unlawful violence mostly within the criminal justice system. Criminal justice is a most sensitive realm and indicative of transgressions of the boundaries drawn by human rights law, democratic and republican institutions. As as in the first study, the specific patterns of egalitarianism will be analysed, as well as structural conditions. Institutional regimes of democracies like e.g. the rule of law, independence of courts, or freedom of the press establish mechanisms of assurance against unlawful and violent interference by the state and by agents of criminal justice institutions in particular; consequently the level of state violence will considerably vary across institutional regimes. Again, the homogenised sample of mature democracies (see above) was mostly used in order to control for institutional mechanisms.

Data

The sample was the same as in the preceding study of punishment. State violence was measured by the Physical Integrity Index which is part of the Cingranelli-Richards Human Rights Database that assesses respect for 13 human rights. David L. Cingranelli and David L. Richards (2007) based their index on the United States State Department Country Reports on Human Rights Practices, which explains the exclusion of the United States from the data. The Physical Integrity Index measures adherence by governments to the first four human rights, and comprises political and extrajudicial killings (since 2001: unlawful or arbitrary deprivation of life), disappearances, torture and political imprisonment. From these a sum score is calculated ranging from 'no government respect for these rights' (0) to 'full government respect for these rights' (8), with each right receiving a rating of one or two. In this study, political imprisonment was excluded in order to achieve a more precise indicator of violence, and consequently the Physical Integrity Index used here has a range from 0 to 6.[4]

---

[4]   For 2005 and 2006, data were directly collected from the Country Reports of the U.S. State Department (http://www.state.gov/g/drl/rls/hrrpt/2005/ and http://www.state.gov/g/drl/rls/hrrpt/2006).

Value patterns were measured in the same way as in the first study. The values of individual autonomy and egalitarianism were complemented by three additional indicators that targeted the divisive nature of meritocratic egalitarianism. These were selected from the four waves of the World Value Survey of 1982, 1990, 1995 and 2000, and measured as the mean percentage of those who supported the respective statements in all waves available in a country. The set of three indicators includes support for large income differences (as above) and support for unrestrained competition. Further, willingness of the public to allow for more interference and simultaneously less egalitarianism was measured as support for the statement that 'greater respect for authority would be a good thing'. Structural inequality and divisions between ethnic groups were the same as in the first study.

Results

Both individualistic and egalitarian values have an impact on state violence, in the total sample (Figures 7 and 8) as well as in the homogenised sample of mature democracies (Figures 9 and 10). The more individual autonomy and non-interference is valued, and the more egalitarian values are adopted, the more state violence in particular in the criminal justice system is restricted, as both the regression line and the comparison of mean levels show. Both values retain their impact even when institutional regimes are in place capable of restraining state violence and violence by agents of criminal justice. As individualism generates respect for the individual and fosters non-interference, and egalitarianism reduces power differentials and supports outreach across group boundaries, both values decrease levels of state violence. Cultural and institutional practices that build on these values shape criminal justice practices, and countries ranking high on both values do guarantee and respect the physical integrity of their citizens, including those who have violated their laws.

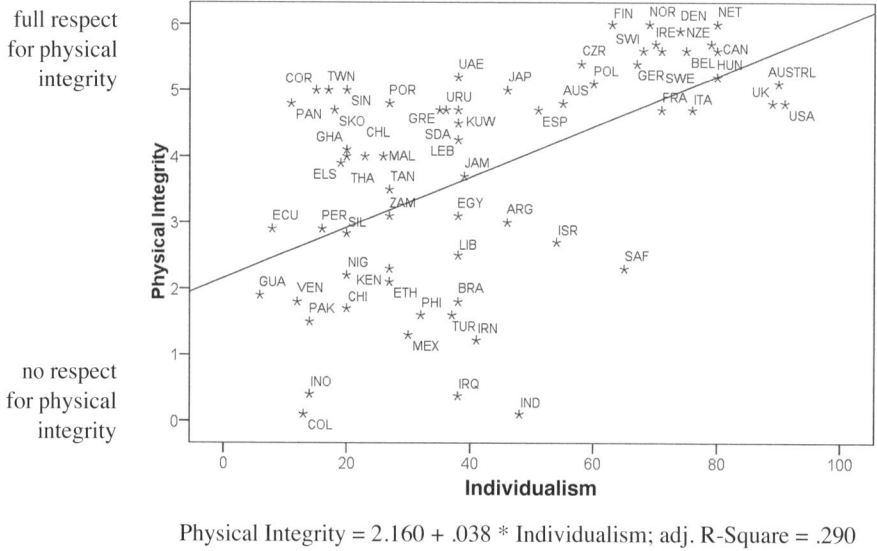

Physical Integrity = 2.160 + .038 * Individualism; adj. R-Square = .290

Figure 7: Individualism and Physical Integrity 1999-2006

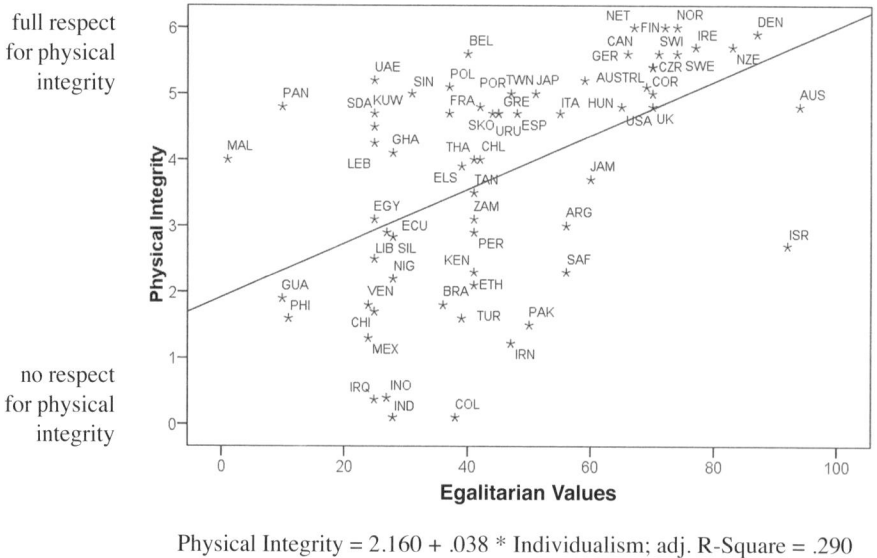

Physical Integrity = 2.160 + .038 * Individualism; adj. R-Square = .290

Figure 8: Egalitarianism and Physical Integrity 1999 – 2006

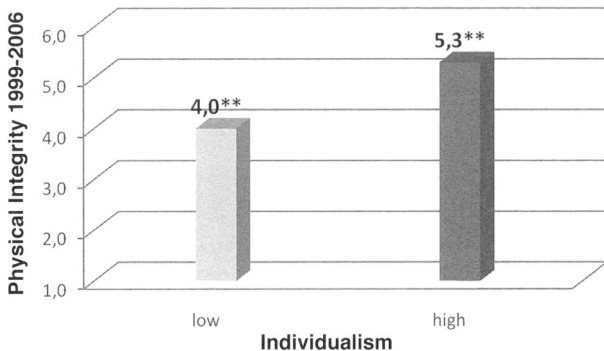

Figure 9: Mature Democracies: Individualism and Physical Integrity 1999 – 2006

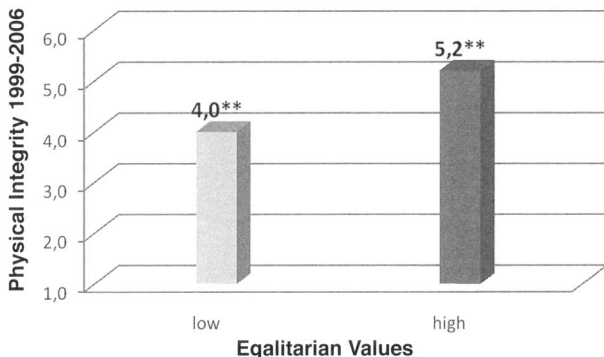

Figure 10: Mature Democracies: Egalitarianism and Physical Integrity 1999 – 2006

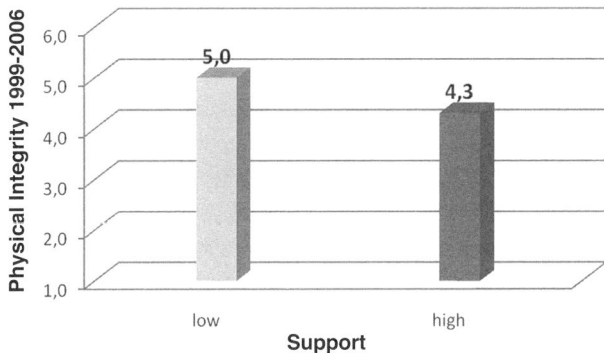

Figure 11: Mature Democracies: Support for More Authority and Physical Integrity 1999 – 2006

In mature democracies the overall impact of value patterns and structural conditions is considerably less strong, given the strength of their institutional regimes.[5] Support for large income differences and unrestrained competition both make state violence significantly more likely (Figure 12 and 13), while support for more authority does not make a difference (Figure 11). Variants of chance oriented and meritocratic egalitarianism, in particular when more divisive forms of competition are supported, increase the level of unlawful violence in the criminal justice system.

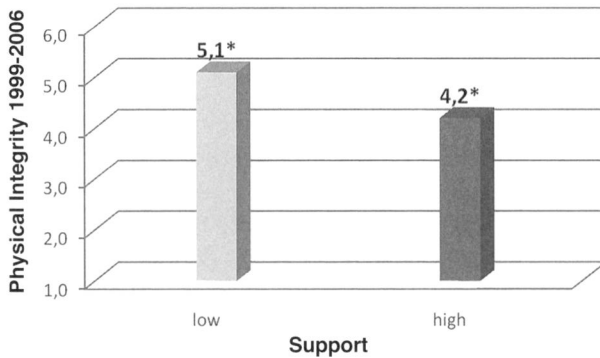

Figure 12: Mature Democracies: Support for Large Income Differences and Physical Integrity 1999 – 2006

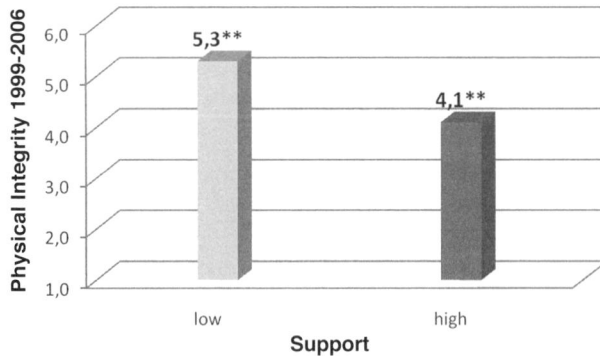

Figure 13: Mature Democracies: Support for Unrestrained Competition and Physical Integrity 1999 – 2006

---

[5] For the total sample the differences are substantial and highly significant.

In mature democracies, income differences and ethnic fractionalization have a smaller impact on the unlawful use of force against citizens than in the total sample (Figures 14 and 15). However, both measures of status difference and inequality demonstrate that even in mature democracies the use of unlawful force by the state is higher where inequality and ethnic fractionalization prevail.

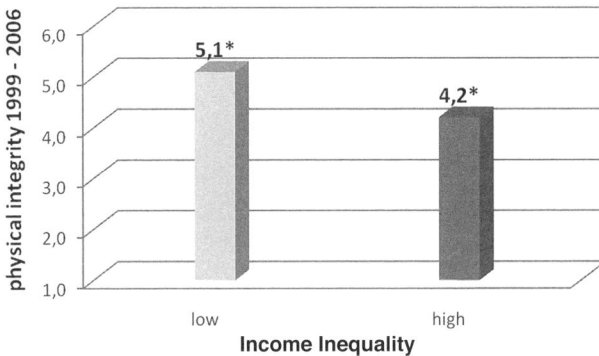

Figure 14: Mature Democracies: Income Inequality and Physical Integrity 1999 – 2006

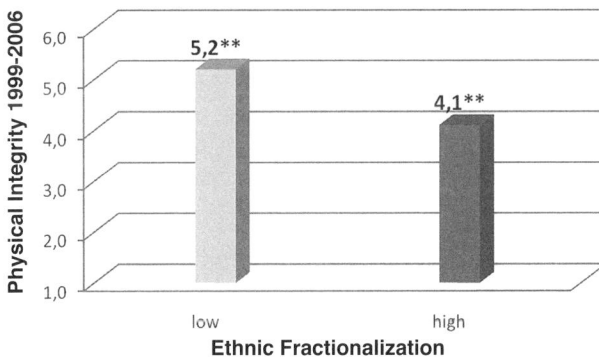

Figure 15: Mature Democracies: Ethnic Fractionalization and Physical Integrity 1999 – 2006

Normative theory, moral visions and penal systems

Both empirical studies were presented as 'tests' of the normative theory of republican justice, as they explored the role of the values on which John Braithwaite's normative theory rests, and assessed these against outcomes and conditions of criminal justice. These were indicated by imprisonment rates and prison conditions, which can be termed as (mostly) lawful interference into the liberties of individuals, whilst the index of state violence mainly measures unlawful violence and interference by criminal justice agencies. However, both coincide where prison conditions become life threatening as this implies unrestricted violence and threat within the prison system itself.

In the 'real world' of governments, criminal justice systems, communities and citizens, the republican values that John Braithwaite sees as foundational for his theory, provide moral visions and an imagination of justice for individuals and communities; they foster institutional regimes that imbue criminal justice with such values; and finally criminal justice expresses and represents these values. The moral vision that a republican theory of criminal justice provides is neither unequivocally achieving better justice, nor more successful in restraining uncontrolled power in the form of unlawful state violence. There was support that both values – autonomy and non-interference into the liberty of individuals, as well as egalitarianism – in principle improve prison conditions, and reduce exertion of unlawful violence in the criminal justice system. However, it was found that a particular version of non-interfering egalitarianism – chance-oriented meritocratic egalitarianism – was linked to deteriorating prison conditions, and higher levels of state violence. In contrast, where the public supported outcome-oriented and more interfering models of egalitarianism, represented mainly by democratic welfare states, prison conditions were significantly better and state violence within criminal justice at lower levels. It comes as a paradox, that decisively non-interfering egalitarianism actually results in more, not less violent state interference. However, this type of egalitarianism allows for and actively endorses debasing status politics and practices for those who fail and who do not play by the rules. These are then realised in particularly poor prison conditions that put offenders 'into their place' and might encourage the use of violence in treating those in the criminal justice system.

Conclusion

The results of the two empirical studies emphasise the importance of equality for a republican theory of justice, and they corroborate Braithwaite's argument that equality is a necessary precondition for both values to flourish and to define the practice of criminal justice systems. First, support for more active and interfering welfare policies, and ostensibly their implementation will improve prison conditions and reduce the use of unlawful violence within criminal justice. Comparative studies and case studies of penal systems in Scandinavian countries (see e.g. Cavadino and Dignan 2006) testify to this. Second, equality and inclusion of different ethnic groups are necessary structural preconditions for improving criminal justice, prison conditions and lawful treatment of citizens within this system. Without equality values and institutions lose power in shaping and improving criminal justice. This becomes obvious in the group of mature democracies which are characterised by a more homogenous institutional structure. Both (income) equality and ethnic equality and ethnic fractionalisation retain their impact in mature democracies with inequality leading to higher imprisonment rates, deteriorating prison conditions and more state violence even under such usually beneficial institutional regimes.

As far as in mature democracies institutional regimes overall foster and embody the two foundational values of republican theory, in particular non-interference into the liberties of individuals, the impact of values, related attitudes and structural conditions on criminal justice tends to be smaller. Both studies therefore strongly support Braithwaite's argument that criminal justice based on a republican theory needs strong, rather than weak institutions, as these can attenuate and mediate structural impact and channel public attitudes and sentiments. Disappointingly, no impact of values on imprisonment could be discerned. Political decisions and legal systems might be the more powerful agents in defining numbers of prisoners (Zimring, Hawkins and Kamin 2001; Zimring and Johnston 2006; van Zyl Smit and Snacken 2009). As a normative theory, republican theory prescribes to use imprisonment as a last resort and to strive for lowest levels of imprisonment (or even abolition) as imprisonment violates the principle of non-interference. In the real world, its foundational values do not make a difference; we need new forms of justice based on these values like e.g. restorative justice that can reduce imprisonment in the long run.

Both empirical studies demonstrate the norms of republican theory in a "tangible fashion", and thus assure us that they are not merely "utopian". Braithwaite has integrated both "concrete and normative aspects" in his republican theory; it is a tool for both, how to keep a critical distance from criminal justice as it is, and how to develop a moral vision of how it should and can be.

References

Alesina, A., Devleeschauwer, A., Easterly, W., Kurlat, S. and Wacziarg, R. (2003): 'Ethnic Fractionalization.' *Journal of Economic Growth* 8:155-194.

Braithwaite, J. (1989): *Crime, Shame and Reintegration*. Cambridge: Cambridge University Press.

Braithwaite, J. (1995a): 'Inequality and Republican Criminology' in J. Hagan and R. Peterson (eds), *Crime and Inequality*, 277-308. Palo Alto: Stanford University Press.

Braithwaite, J. (1995b): 'Community Values and Australian Jurisprudence.' *Sydney Law Review* 17: 351-372.

Braithwaite, J. (1995c): 'Corporate Crime and Republican Criminological Praxis.' In F. Pearce and L.Snyder (eds), *Ethics, Law and State*. Toronto: University of Toronto Press.

Braithwaite, J. (1997): 'On Speaking Softly and Carrying Sticks: Neglected Dimensions of Republican Separation of Powers' *University of Toronto Law Journal* 47: 1-57.

Braithwaite, J. (1998): 'Institutionalizing Distrust, Enculturating Trust' in V. Braithwaite and M. Levi (eds), *Trust and Governance*, 343 – 375. New York: Russell Sage Foundation.

Braithwaite, J. (2000): 'Republican Theory, the Good Society and Crime Control' in S. Karstedt and K. Bussmann (eds), *Social Dynamics of Crime and Control* , 85-104. Oxford: Hart Publishing.

Braithwaite J. (2002): *Restorative Justice and Responsive Regulation*. Oxford: Oxford University Press.

Braithwaite, J. and Drahos, P. (2000): *Global Business Regulation*. Cambridge: Cambridge University Press.

Braithwaite, J. and Pettit, P. (1990): *Not Just Deserts. A Republican Theory of Criminal Justice*. Oxford: Oxford University Press.

Braithwaite, J. and Pettit, P. (2000): 'Republicanism and Restorative Justice: An Explanatory and Normative Connection' in H. Strang and J. Braithwaite (eds), *Restorative Justice. Philosophy to Practice*. Aldershot: Ashgate.

Caldeira, T. P. R. and Holston, J. (1999): 'Democracy and Violence in Brazil.' *Comparative Studies in Society and History* 41: 691-729.

Cavadino, M. and Dignan, J. (2006): *Penal Systems. A Comparative Approach*. London: Sage.

Cingranelli, D. L. and Richards, D. L. (2007): The Cingranelli-Richards (CIRI) Human Rights Dataset, Data Version: 2007.04.12, [http://humanrightsdata.org].

Donnelly, J. (1985): *The Concept of Human Rights*. London and Sydney: Croom Helm.

Freedom House (1973-2009): *Freedom in the World. Country Ratings and Status by Region, FIW 1973-2009*. Aggregate Data Excel File http://www.freedomhouse. org/uploads/fiw09/CompHistData/FIW_ScoresByRegion.xls.

Fund for Peace (2005-2009): Failed States index (FSI). http://www.fundforpeace.org/ web/index.php?option=com_content&task=view&id=99&Itemid=323

Goldston, J.A. (1999): 'Race Discrimination in Europe: Problems and Prospects.' *European Human Rights Law Review* 5: 457-472.

Hofstede, G. and Hofstede, G. J. (eds) (2005): *Cultures and Organizations. Software of the Mind*. Revised and Expanded 2nd Edition. New York: MacGraw-Hill Professional.

Ishay, M.R. (2004): 'What are Human Rights? Six Historical Controversies.' *Journal of Human Rights* 3: 359-371.

Jaggers, K. and Gurr, T. (1995): 'Tracking Democracy's Third Wave With the Polity III Data.' *Journal of Peace Research* 32: 469-482.

Karstedt, S. (2006): 'Democracy, Values and Violence: Paradoxes, Tensions, and Comparative Advantages of Liberal Inclusion.' *Annals of the American Academy of Political and Social Science*, 605: 50-81.

Koskienniemi, M. (2005): *From apology to utopia. The structure of international legal argument*. Cambridge: Cambridge University Press.

Kuhn, P.W. (1999): *The cultural study of law: Reconstructing legal scholarship*. Chicago: University of Chicago Press.

Mann, M. (2005): *The dark side of democracy. Explaining ethnical cleansing*. Cambridge: Cambridge University Press.

Marshall, M. G. and Jaggers, K. (2005): *Polity IV Data Set*. Center for International Development and Conflict Management, College Park: University of Maryland. http://www.systemicpeace.org/inscr/inscr.htm (Version: p4v2008)

Mead, H. (1964): The Psychology of Punitive Justice. In: Reck, A. J. (ed): *Selected Writings*. 212-239. Chicago: University of Chicago Press.

Mendez, J. E. (1999): 'Problems of Lawless Violence: Introduction.' In: J.E. Mendez, G. O'Donnell, and P.S. Pinheiro (eds), *The (un)rule of law and the underprivileged in Latin America*. 1 – 25. Notre Dame: University of Notre Dame Press.

Mendez, E., O'Donnell, G. and Pinheiro, P.S. (eds) (1999): *The (un)rule of law and the underprivileged in Latin America*. Notre Dame: University of Notre Dame Press.

Neapolitano, J.L. (2001): 'An Examination of Cross-National Variation in Punitiveness.' *International Journal of Offender Therapy and Comparative Criminology* 45: 691-710.

Triandis, H. C. and Trafimov, D. (2001): 'Cross-national prevalence of collectivism' In: C. Sedikides and M.B. Brewer (eds): *Individual self, relational self, collective self*. 245-276. Ann Arbor: Taylor and Francis.

United Nations Development Programme (UNDP) (2002): *Human Development Report 2002. Deepening Democracy in a Fragmented World*. New York, Oxford: Oxford University Press. http://hdr.undp.org/en/media/HDR_2002_EN_ Complete.pdf.

US State Department (1999-2006): *Human Rights: Country Reports*. Washington, http://www.state.gov/g/drl/rls/hrrpt.

Walmsley, R. (1999-2009): *World Prison Population List* (1-8). London. http://www. prisonstudies.org.

Whitman, J. (2003): *Harsh Justice. Criminal Punishment and the Widening Divide between America and Europe*. Oxford: Oxford University Press.

Zimring, F., Hawkins, G. and Kamin, S. (2001): *Punishment and Democracy: Three Strikes and You are Out in California*. Oxford: Oxford University Press.

Zimring, F. and Johnson, D. T. (2006): 'Public Opinion and the Governance of Punishment in Democratic Political Systems.' In S. Karstedt and G. LaFree, (eds): *Democracy, Crime and Justice*. The Annals of the American Academy of Political and Social Science 605: 266-280.

van Zyl Smit, D. and Snacken, S. (2009): *Principles of European Prison Law and Policy*. Oxford: Oxford University Press.

WHY CRIMINOLOGY NEEDS OUTSIDERS

Tom Daems

Introduction

Most readers are probably familiar with the FAQ-sections (Frequently Asked Questions) of brochures or webpages of government organisations and private companies. The rationale is simple: the most common questions are grouped together in a simple format – standard questions are followed by standard answers. It is a smart way to avoid getting too many questions either by (proactively) anticipating difficulties that might arise when citizens or customers are in need of more information about a certain service or a specific product, or (reactively) by way of past experience with getting too many questions on a certain issue that, apparently, is in need of further clarification. The bottom-line is that it is a useful and often-practised technique to reduce the workload and to save money. Questions and answers are streamlined into a framework that is easy to read and to consult. It is, in addition, a way to deter people: all too often you first have to consult the FAQ-section before calling, writing or e-mailing to your service provider. If you fail to do this, you run the risk of receiving the friendly request that you should first study the FAQ before your particular question is allowed to receive a personalized answer.

Readers of this chapter may also know from experience that phone, internet, gas and electricity companies are quite good at the FAQ-game. Moreover, they often add an extra obstacle to discourage callers to ask those questions that do not fit the FAQ-format: long waiting lines to get someone to talk to you at the helpdesk ('all our operators are busy at the moment, please wait ...'). A symphony of Beethoven that, at other times, might be a guarantee for relaxing or inspiring moments suddenly turns into an irritating tune. As a caller you also realize that such companies often out-source their help-desks to call-centres where underpaid and unexperienced employees aim to cope with a disproportionate work-load, and where their productivity is closely being monitored (and sanctioned) in terms of the number of calls being handled in a certain time slot. FAQ (and long waiting lines) are, therefore, all too often, and regrettably, ways to avoid questions; in particular those questions that fall out of the mainstream, that is, those questions that are in need of time, that deserve to be treated with more diligence and expertise than is being permitted by the limited and pre-determined amount of time reserved per call. Diversion may not always be the principal operation of our criminal justice systems, yet it certainly is at the heart of how we are being treated day-in day-out by providers of key services that are indispensable to make life possible in contemporary societies.

Sometimes also criminology is like FAQ: a pre-channeled and pre-programmed practice that is not about asking questions but rather about producing ready-made and predictable answers in a time period that is, preferably, as short as possible. This chapter, however, is not devoted to FAQ-criminology - even though FAQ-criminology will inevitably loom at the background of our discussion. Rather we pay tribute to the persistent caller, the customer who is able to file his complaint about his bills or about his malfunctioning internet-connection and who, audaciously, manages to beat the Xth re-run of the Yth symphony of Beethoven. It is our contention that the work of John Braithwaite often pierces through the thick walls of FAQ-criminology and this also explains why we devote some attention to this topic in our chapter.

The central argument of this chapter is that criminology needs outsiders. However, we do not use the word 'outsiders' here to refer to the raw material of criminology, the stuff that criminology works with (deviants, criminals, delinquents, troubled youth, …), but rather to label those criminologists who invite us to take some distance from our daily work as criminologists. Outsiders, then, are those criminologists who are well aware of the fact that the stuff we work with, and the questions that we routinely ask and aim (or are asked) to address, are at the centre of public debate and social policy. However, the nature of the questions that such outsiders ask about what we as criminologists do (and about how we present that action to ourselves and the world around us), aims to promote a degree of self-awareness that is indispensable for a science like criminology – at least if we agree that criminology should not be a science populated by one-eyed cyclops. This also implies that such questions are often uncomfortable ones – but, obviously, that is exactly the reason why they tend to escape the strait-jacket of FAQ.

In the next sections we will aim to clarify this. In section two we briefly discuss the views on criminology expressed by five such outsiders: Stanley Cohen, Nils Christie, Louk Hulsman, David Garland and John Braithwaite. In section three we speculate about the reasons that can explain why criminology, despite the critical views that are being expressed by such outsiders, still considers them to be core members of our criminological family. Indeed, it is remarkable to observe that those who have the most critical opinion about our discipline, tend to be so warmly embraced in the centre of criminology: is this a matter of mere masochism or is there more going on? In section four we will further elaborate the need for an external view on criminology by briefly discussing and criticizing Foucault's views on criminology. We will argue that the power/knowledge framework is a fruitful way to cultivate an external view on criminology but that, at the same time, it does not fully capture the many ways in which criminological knowledge impacts upon the world around us. In sections five and six we will illustrate what a more wide-ranging external view on criminology may look like by briefly discussing some recent research on restorative justice against the background of what some sociologists have termed a 'therapy culture'.

Five outsiders

Few readers would disagree when we write that Stanley Cohen is one of the most inspiring criminologists of our times. Yet, when Cohen published a book in 1988 he gave it the title *Against Criminology*. On the first page of the book the reader encounters a strong quote by Adorno: 'One must belong to a tradition to hate it properly'. In the opening chapter Cohen mused about his difficult relationship to criminology, which he termed (inspired by Marcuse) 'repressive tolerance': "Every attempt I have ever made to distance myself from the subject, to criticize it, even to question its very right to exist, has only got me more involved in its inner life" (Cohen 1988: 8). Sometimes his critique was quite harsh as, for example, in the closing lines of a paper devoted to abolitionism: "(…) abolitionism is a 'thought experiment': the type of critical opposition to accepted modes of thinking that intellectuals should provide instead of the corrupted technicism of such disciplines as criminology" (Cohen 1991: 739). At other moments his tone was more ironic, for example in a paper discussing the academic ritual of conference life. Here he explained why criminology conferences supplied his main data-set for the paper as follows: "As long as governments, foundations and research councils retain their touching faith that the crime problem can be solved by getting people together in hotels to talk about it, these will be rich sources for replication research" (Cohen 1997: 69). In *Against Criminology* Cohen reflected on the ambivalent relationship between outsiders and the mainstream, and how, paradoxically, the outsiders move back to the centre of criminology: "The more successful our attack on the old regime, the more we received Ph.D.'s, tenure, publisher's contracts, and research funds, appeared on booklists and examination questions, and even became directors of institutes of criminology and received awards from professional associations" (Cohen 1988: 8).

The same applies to thinkers such as Nils Christie and Louk Hulsman. When Christie was invited in Sheffield, in March 1976, to give an opening lecture in order to celebrate the establishment of its criminology institute, he observed the following: "Maybe we should not have any criminology. Maybe we should rather abolish institutes, not open them. Maybe the social consequences of criminology are more dubious than we like to think" (Christie 1977: 1). Christie used the word 'maybe' three times but this was rather a sign of politeness to his welcoming hosts than an expression of sincere doubt. Indeed, that hesitance would quickly disappear: "My suspicion is that criminology to some extent has amplified a process where conflicts have been taken away from the parties directly involved and thereby have either disappeared or become other people's property. In both cases a deplorable outcome" (Christie 1977: 1). Two decades later Christie further elaborated his critique of the functioning of criminology as follows: "Long reports of the obvious. Repetitions. Elaborate calculations leading to what we all knew. How can it be like this? How come that so much criminology is dull, tedious and intensely empty as to new insights?" (Christie 1997: 13). According to Christie criminology had become dull, tedious, and empty of new insights because of the oversocialization of criminologists: the university system, as it currently functions, and the availability of large data sets compiled by state organizations turn us into children, who are no longer able to think for ourselves and, in particular, who are no longer able to think 'out-of-the-crime-box'.

This is a critique that also returns in the work of Louk Hulsman: "Crime has no ontological reality. Crime is not the *object* but the *product* of criminal policy. Criminalisation is one of the many ways to construct social reality" (Hulsman 1986: 71). The problem with criminology, so Hulsman argued, is that it often is unable to take an external view on how social reality is being constructed by means of concepts such as 'crime'. Interestingly, and in line with what Christie writes on the oversocialization of criminologists, also Hulsman pointed to the key role of university education in this respect. In the opening pages of an unpublished syllabus that he used for his classes Hulsman argued that students should not merely learn how to 'read' a map but rather, and foremost, how to 'construct' a map. University teachers, therefore, have to abstain from offering a ready-made map to their students and incite them to find their own way in the different domains of social reality (Hulsman 1980: 1-2).

Already at the start of his career David Garland argued that criminology was originally "a discourse fixed in a socio-political space, a technical auxiliary of the welfare state, which endlessly reproduces itself and the policies it supports" (Garland 1985: 30, note 33). In 1997 he argued that we should think about criminology as a "(…) *practical* ingredient in the modern system of penal control (…) one of the discourses upon which penal practice is based, one of the knowledges that combines with penal power to create our modern system of penal control" (Garland 1997: 182). And most recently, at the occasion of a plenary speech in July 2008 in Barcelona, where Garland addressed a large audience of criminologists attending the XVth World Congress of the International Society for Criminology, he confirmed that, in his view, "(…) criminology is intimately (at the *epistemological* level) and directly (at the *social* level) tied into government (…). Criminology's social status continues to rest in large part upon its practical utility and its value for government" (Garland 2008: 25; for more details, see Daems 2008).

And last but not least, also Braithwaite, whose contribution to criminology is being honoured throughout this book, has in the past not been so friendly to criminology. In the first chapter of his important book *Crime, shame and reintegration*, under the heading 'Criminology as cause of crime?', he wondered "(...) whether the professionalization of the study of crime is part of a wider social movement which has tended further to debilitate the social response to crime, rather than strengthen it". Braithwaite was critical of how American criminology became an export product, claiming to solve crime problems in the Third World whereas its domestic achievements were far from laudable. And, so he added, "[P]rofessional criminology, in all its major variants, can be unhelpful in maintaining a social climate appropriate to crime control because in different ways its thrust is to professionalize, systematize, scientize, and de-communitize justice" (Braithwaite 1989: 5-6).

Why do we need outsiders?

These criticisms are particularly harsh: criminologists are variously described as corrupted technicists, thieves, creatures who produce dull and tedious 'insights'; criminologists are depicted as rats in a Foucauldian power/ knowledge race and they are even held responsible for a crime problem that they often aim to eradicate. For some criminologists (especially those amongst us without an elephant's skin) such comments might be experienced as extremely painful. To others (who are more combative) they might sound as a deep insult: why should we swallow this? The most obvious response would be to excommunicate such outsiders from our inner-group. A cyclist who dares to ride the *tour de France* on EPO or a weightlifter who pumps huge quantities of anabolic steroids into his body at the Olympics are promptly expelled from further competition. Why not apply similar sanctions in the world of science?

However, that does not seem to be the normal way of processing the deviants that we discussed in the previous section: we do not banish them from our collective criminological memory and we do not banish them from our lecture rooms. On the contrary, we tend to do the opposite: we invite them to open our criminology institutes and to give major plenary lectures at our most important conferences; we offer them the opportunity to write papers for the (inaugural) issues of our most valued criminology journals; and we celebrate their careers by offering them life time achievement awards and honorary doctorates. And, remarkably, we do all this to honour their contributions to criminology. What can explain this strange behaviour?

In this section we suggest four reasons that can account for our somewhat strange behaviour. However, we want to stress at the outset that this is a speculative exercise: we do not have any empirical material that suggests that A, B, C or D is, factually, the most appropriate explanation. We will argue, however, that the last option is, in our view, the most attractive one. But this is the case for normative rather than for empirical reasons - because we would *like* that explanation to be the one that prevails rather than because it *is* like that.

The first two reasons are the least sophisticated: either criminologists act as masochists who (as if being immersed in a never-ending sexually devious act of S/M) are eager to receive some spanking or whipping that gives them some pleasure, or they are not able to identify the hard edge of the attacks that the outsiders whom we discussed in the previous section, launch at our discipline. Either they like it (maybe in view of criminology's intellectual history which is characterized by seemingly never-ending discussions on what criminology should be about?) or they do not fully realize what exactly is happening to them (maybe because they are too preoccupied with their own FAQ-criminology and, therefore, they do not have the time nor the energy to read in-depth and absorb what such outsiders write about criminology?). Both explanations are plausible candidates, for sure, but certainly not the most attractive ones.

The third explanation is more cynical in nature. It suggests that criminologists tend to be close followers of the prescription embedded in an old saying 'Keep your friends close, keep your enemies closer'. From this perspective, it makes for example sense to elect a president for one of our professional societies (such as the American, British, European, Dutch or Flemish Society of Criminology) from the group of outsiders or it can explain why we sometimes give an award to one of the outsiders. Such decisions, then, would be inspired by strategic reasons: it conveys the message to the outside world that criminology strives to be an open, self-critical discipline but, underneath the surface, one senses and fears that it is business as usual. If the four previous presidents (and the next five ones) are elected from more mainstream circles and if the majority of awards (or the major awards) go to more mainstream criminologists, then there is no damage done. Occasionally electing a president from the outsiders or occasionally celebrating the career of one of them, then, becomes a (Machiavellian) strategy to domesticate the outsider's voice: one creates an image of a professional community that takes the outsiders seriously but deep inside the clever observer realizes that it is mostly about impression-management and appeasing the deviant constituents: 'Look, we gave you A, and we elected B, now it is up to C, D, E, F, G, H,…and Z to get their share of the cake'. We can imagine that readers who are familiar with the recent history of criminology may have some examples in mind that may support the validity of this third explanation. However, as we discussed before, our exercise is speculative in nature and, from a normative perspective, this option is obviously, like the two previous ones, not a very attractive one.

The fourth explanation is the most appealing one. It suggests that we embrace the views of such 'outsiders' not because of masochistic, agnostic or strategic reasons, but rather because they offer us a reflection on criminology which we perceive to be indispensable to our discipline, and which can be termed an external view on criminology: a reflection on what criminologists do, what they claim to do, and what the implications of our activities are for the world we are living in. These kinds of reflection, this way of looking at our very own activities and our very own profession, are highly important: they are about bending back on our deepest assumptions and daily practices. They provide, therefore, an antidote to the ever-present risk that criminology becomes cyclopical, that is, that we turn into one-eyed creatures who are exclusively focused on our day-to-day preoccupations and the questions that we want (or have) to address. In short, it is an antidote to the risk of losing sight of the bigger picture. An external view is necessary in order to cultivate using that second eye that puts things into perspective and into a broader context.

That is the reason why we need (normatively speaking) the outsiders that we discussed in the previous section and that is (hopefully) the reason why we, despite their often deeply uncomfortable views, welcome such outsiders back in the centre of criminology.

Foucault's external view on criminology, its strengths and its limits

One interesting and promising angle to cultivate such an external view on criminology, is that of the sociology of punishment. The major innovation of Michel Foucault's (1977) *Discipline and Punish* was not so much that he gave a boost to thinking about the birth of the prison in new ways. In the end, revisionist history writing on punishment and control was already on the rise since the late 1960s and attracted further attention throughout the 1970s, and, obviously, as Foucault himself also acknowledged, Rusche and Kirchheimer's (1939) pioneering work *Punishment and Social Structure* was already published in the late 1930s. Rather it was the way in which Foucault wove criminology into his overall narrative, that made his study so original and thought-provoking. The prison became a laboratory for observation and documentation and provided the appropriate conditions in which a science of criminology could emerge. Criminology, in turn, would contribute to an enhancement and refinement of technologies of power. Within the penitentiary apparatus the convicted offender was being transformed into the "delinquent' who '(…) is to be distinguished from the offender by the fact that it is not so much his act as his life that is relevant in characterizing him" (Foucault 1977: 251). Crime, then, is being transformed into a technical problem and better techniques of intervention would, eventually, 'cure' the delinquent and lead to his normalization. For Foucault criminology has never been able to break out of the power/knowledge cage. Indeed, his opinion on the scientific status of modern criminology was utterly dismissive. In one of his many interviews, in a passage that is quite well-known to many criminologists, he expressed his views as follows:

> "Have you ever read any criminological texts? They are staggering. And I say this out of astonishment, not aggressiveness, because I fail to comprehend how the discourse of criminology has been able to go on at this level. One has the impression that it is of such utility, is needed so urgently and rendered so vital for the working of the system, that it does not even need to seek a theoretical justification for itself, or even simply a coherent framework. It is entirely utilitarian." (Foucault 1980: 47)

We would like to make two observations on these views of Foucault: one supportive and one critical comment. The supportive observation goes as follows: by establishing a link between knowledge and power, between criminology and penal regimes, Foucault opened new avenues to study the various relationships between penal and control developments on the one hand, and the origins, development and operation of criminology on the other hand. He therefore helped cultivate a particular way to perceive criminology from an external perspective, in the sense of the fourth option that we discussed in the previous section. Foucault's approach towards criminology has in particular inspired two of the outsiders whom we discussed in section two: Stanley Cohen and David Garland. However, there is also a problem with such a Foucauldian view on criminology, in particular if it comes to dominate the full range of options to think about criminology's impact upon the wider world. Because Foucault wanted to come to terms with the modern-day prison as a disciplinary institution he focused on the birth of a specific clinical, treatment-oriented criminology in nineteenth century prisons and he solely examined the operation of criminology in relation to its potential for control. Other aspects were left out of the picture. The same applies to David Garland's (2001) understanding of criminology in *The Culture of Control*: because Garland is interested in the *practical* effects of criminology in the *constitution* of the culture of control he leaves those that have only played a marginal role in this respect, out of the picture (Daems 2008). In the remainder of this section we will further elaborate this critique. We will use the example of victimology to argue that knowledge can impact in different ways on our responses to crime: the power/knowledge frame is, for sure, an important one, but it does not capture the many ways in which knowledge shapes our reactions to crime.

It is possible to perceive the origins and an important part of the historical development of criminology as revolving around three questions about the criminal population that have to do with identification, etiology and policy: Who are they? Why do they commit crime? And how to reduce crime? In her study *Kriminologie im Deutschen Kaiserreich*, which deals with the history of criminology in the German *Kaiserreich* (1880-1914), historian Silviana Galassi (2004) documents at length how, since the early 1880s, crime developments became visible nation-wide. A true avalanche of numbers revealed crime as a mass phenomenon and incited the imagination of the early criminologists. At the same time, attempts were made to move onto other vocabularies: the moral tone in speaking about crime and its control shifted (at least at the surface) to a scientific one. Indeed, the science of the criminal needed to compete with, and disconnect itself from, other ways of framing the problem of crime, such as those inspired by religion (the divine order and its 'sinners'), philosophy (the social contract and its 'breachers'), politics (the worldly order and its 'enemies'). Medical practitioners and legal scholars played an important role in the pioneering reflections on crime and its causation. Some of them (such as Krafft-Ebings, Bleuler, Kraepelin, Sommer, Gaupp and Koch) rejected Lombroso's atavism but remained faithful to the idea of the born criminal which they linked to the theory of degeneration which flourished between 1894 and 1904. Others (such as von Liszt and Aschaffenburg) also rejected the idea of the born criminal and were in favour of what Galassi terms a *Vereinigungstheorie*: criminals were deemed to be 'degenerated individuals' and as such predisposed to crime, yet their actual crimes were seen as resulting from 'external influences'.

In the past decades the same kind of questions that animated the early criminologists have been asked about another group, that is, victims of crime: Who are they? Why do people become victims? And how to reduce victimization? Victim surveys, theoretical and empirical developments in victimology, and victimization prevention initiatives have, to an important extent, changed the criminological and crime policy landscape. Some of this knowledge about victims of crime is, for sure, useful in terms of crime control and has informed, for example, innovative prevention projects such as those aimed at tackling repeat victimization. Adopting a Foucauldian power/knowledge approach is, therefore, possible and fruitful (Daems 2005). However, such knowledge also has brought a different dimension of rule-breaking into view and, accordingly, inspired responses that are not so much useful in terms of controlling crime but rather for other reasons.

One of the crucial innovations is that the various needs of victims came to be mapped: victims want a less formal process where their views count; victims want more information about both the processing and outcome of their cases; victims want to participate in their cases; victims want to be treated respectfully and fairly; victims want material restoration; victims want emotional restoration and an apology (Strang 2002: 8-23). Victimologists started to speak about 'secondary victimization' to denote the negative experiences victims of crime were (and are) having when being confronted with a cold criminal justice system that lacks empathy for their plight. This inspired a set of responses to make criminal justice systems and their professionals more sensitive to the predicament of victims of crime (such as victim services, victims' rights, compensation schemes, and so forth). More recently, also the 'primary victimization' has received much more attention in responses to criminal victimization. This can be illustrated for the case of recent research on restorative justice. A specific kind of scientific knowledge about victims (pertaining to their fears, sense of alienation, post-traumatic stress symptoms and so forth), is being mobilized to assess to what extent restorative interventions perform better in producing certain desired 'victim effects' in terms of recovery and emotional restoration (Daems 2010).

The point we aim to make, therefore, is the following: the fact that victimology is often not useful in terms of crime control does not necessarily imply that it had no impact on penal and control developments. The Foucauldian conception of criminology forecloses a discussion of criminologies that are further away, or even disconnected, from penal control. The focus on 'control criminologies' obscures how various forms of knowledge may have impacted in different ways – less or even unrelated to control - on punishment itself. A sociology of punishment that solely thinks of knowledge in relation to control fails to capture that, in cases of criminal victimization, offenders also might be addressed as victimizers. In those cases, then, other forms of knowledge, other experts, and other expectations tend to enter the game. Cultivating an external view on criminology, therefore, implies that we open our eyes to the different ways in which criminological knowledge impacts upon the world around us. Moreover, this will also direct our attention to other dimensions of our societies, and the ways in which criminological knowledge becomes operative in different ways.

In the remainder of this chapter we will illustrate this need for a more wide-ranging framework to think about the uses of criminology by means of a brief reflection on recent research on restorative justice, an area that Braithwaite has done so much to develop. But in line with our aim to further develop ways in which the sociology of punishment can open fruitful and promising ways to stimulate such an external view on criminology, we will first discuss the background against which we will elaborate an external view on restorative justice research.

The silent response to 9/11

We usually associate the aftermath of the tragic events of 11 September 2001 with a wave of law enforcement initiatives and surveillance measures: the American Patriot Act; the stringent security regulations at airports and the targeting of 'suspicious' individuals; the global-wide war against terrorism; the prison base at Guantánamo Bay; the military invasions of Afghanistan, Iraq; and so forth. It would be a mistake, however, to see 9/11 as the starting-point of a new era of surveillance in western societies. In his book *Surveillance after September 11* David Lyon argued that the new surveillance measures were "(…) just surface symptoms of deeper and longer-term shifts in political culture, governance and social control, not only in North America but throughout the world". Many of the 'deeper shifts', therefore, "(…) were already in process, and 9/11 served simply to accelerate their arrival in a more public way" (Lyon 2003: 3-4).

However, there was also another set of responses to 9/11 that has received much less attention. In the introduction to their book *L'Empire du traumatisme. Enquête sur la condition de victime* Didier Fassin and Richard Rechtman (2007) highlight the grand scale of interventions related to mental health care after the attacks on the Twin Towers in New York City. About 9,000 mental health specialists, including 700 psychiatrists, intervened to give psychological support to survivors, witnesses and inhabitants. Numerous internet websites, surveys, and scholarly conferences were devoted to the traumatic impact of the events. These were not only concerned with survivors or witnesses but also with those who watched the images on television. The term 'trauma' also came to be used in a more expanded sense, that is, America was a 'traumatized nation'. In view of the massive scale of violence of the attacks, this response, and its psychological framing, was perceived to be so self-evident and normal that nobody was questioning it (Fassin & Rechtman 2007: 12). However, so Fassin and Rechtman argue, this response was far from self-evident. A quarter of a century ago hardly anybody (with the exception of some closed circles of psychiatrists and psychologists) tended to speak in terms of traumatisation, and also the large-scale crisis- and after-care interventions by mental-health professionals, were almost non-existent. Over the past 25 years these have become, slowly but surely, part of the standard response to many similar events. Like Lyon (2003) who insists on the continuities between pre- and post-9/11 developments related to surveillance, so Fassin and Rechtman (2007) argue against making the response to the 'trauma' of 9/11 the starting-point of a new era in mental health care: its roots need to be situated in the early 1980s.

The book by Fassin and Rechtman is one of the most recent additions to a growing literature on how concerns with mental health have come to the fore in recent times. One of the decisive moments that scholars working in this field of research regularly point at, is the inclusion of PTSD (Post

Traumatic Stress Disorder) in 1980 in DSM III, after a successful campaign of traumatized Vietnam veterans and their supporters in the late 1970s (Scott 1990). PTSD quickly became a highly successful and closely studied diagnosis. A conservative count yielded more than 16,000 publications by 1999 (Summerfield 2001: 95). An editor of the *American Journal of Psychiatry* observed in 1995, somewhat ironically, that PTSD is the only psychiatric diagnosis that patients want to have (Rechtman 2004: 914). The attractivity of PTSD is partly explainable by the fact that it, uniquely, supposes a single cause:

> "The entire canon of diagnostic categories in DSM IV is phenomenological and descriptive, bar post-traumatic stress disorder. Aetiology is not included in definitions because it is invariably multifactorial. Only post-traumatic stress disorder supposes a single cause (...) What makes the disorder preferred to other potential diagnoses is the term 'post-traumatic' in its name, which seems to 'prove' a direct aetiological link between the present and an index event in the past that excludes other factors'" (Summerfield 2001: 97).

Rechtman adds the following reflection which may help clarify why PTSD has been so successful and why it became so widely diagnosed: "Nothing before or during the event can lead to moral suspicion, and there is no way of blaming the victim. One could say that this is the logical consequence of the external aetiology of this specific disorder. As this pathology is exclusively created by an external event outside the range of normal human experience, there can be no reason for blaming the victim" (Rechtman 2004: 914). According to Rechtman PTSD has to a large extent contributed to the recognition of the suffering of victims of all kinds of stressful events but, so he adds, they have paid a price for this, that is, "(…) a reconfiguration of this *condition of victim*, in which a *human condition* – being a victim – has come to be locked into a *clinical condition* – suffering from a *PTSD*" (Rechtman 2002: 778, my translation).

The price, then, is that human suffering comes to be captured in a specific language and framework of understanding: when there is a stressful event and the symptoms are identified, then suffering, according to the logic of PTSD, is equalled with traumatisation. There is a growing critical literature on how this way of reasoning has impacted upon international interventions in war-affected countries. During the 1990s the psychological effect of war on populations became a major preoccupation and various psychosocial programmes were promoted to facilitate psychological healing. This stands in sharp contrast with earlier humanitarian interventions which hardly took healing war trauma as a target and tended to override other and, arguably, often more pressing needs of people in post-conflict situations, that is, rebuilding communities, schools, basic infrastructure, economic activity, and so forth. Pupavac speaks of an 'international therapeutic governance' which "(…) pathologizes war-affected populations as psychologically dysfunctional. As such they are deemed to lack the capacity for self-government without extensive external management to break intergenerational cycles of psychosocial dysfunction" (Pupavac 2004: 378).

Pupavac's critique, as she stresses, is not meant to deny that people are marked by experiences but is directed at how current thinking presumes universal vulnerability and the necessity of intervention at the expense of resilience and survivorship. Moreover, this 'therapeutic governance' often does not take into account how people in war-affected nations understand and experience their suffering and how they respond to it: the Western therapeutic model is supplanted to such regions without having regard to culture-specific coping strategies and positive capacities for self-government (see Pupavac 2002; Pupavac 2004). This is also why some have warned against using PTSD in non-Western war-affected countries: the category is built upon Western-based assumptions of individuality which are often not shared in those countries and, therefore, it tends to emphasize similarities in responses to trauma while underestimating the differences between cultural groups. As a result, also the assumption that individual treatment strategies developed in the West can be transferred to non-Western settings has been seriously questioned (see e.g. Bracken *et al.* 1995; Summerfield 1999).

Sociologists such as Nolan (1998) and Furedi (2004) have argued that preoccupations with mental health issues are not restricted to large-scale terrorist attacks or post-war zones but have pervaded western cultures that tend to elevate emotional well-being to a most precious good. They speak of 'therapeutic states' and 'therapy cultures'. Crucial thereby is that the cultural understanding of behaviours and experiences tends to change. As Furedi notes: "(…) therapeutics does not simply reflect uncertainties (…) it also cultivates a distinct orientation towards the world. It sensitises people to regard a growing range of their experiences as victimising and as traumatizing" (Furedi 2004: 129). Also for Furedi the response to the attacks of 9/11 exemplified the influence of the therapeutic:

"The guidance offered to the public was underwritten by the conviction that most Americans required some form of therapeutic instruction to come to terms with the tragedy. This literature was informed by the assumption that intervention on an unprecedented scale would be necessary to deal with the psychological consequences of 9/11" (Furedi 2004: 13).

A culture becomes therapeutic, so Furedi argues, "(…) when this form of thinking expands from informing the relationship between the individual and therapist to shaping public perceptions about a variety of issues" (Furedi 2004: 22; see also Fassin & Rechtman 2007: 18). A therapy culture provides scripts through which people come to understand themselves and their relationships with others. They solve problems and they face challenges through a therapeutic lens. Dramatic episodes in life, then, are made sense of in mental health terms, and coping with painful encounters is being influenced by prevailing therapeutic frameworks. This does not imply that these authors see *le traumatisme* or therapy culture as the sole cultural force impinging on people. Rather they aim to highlight how a new language, new frameworks, new forms of expertise, and so forth have become available and impact upon self-understanding and social organization.

In the last section of this chapter we will argue that criminological research on restorative justice plays a part in making available and supporting such a new language, frameworks and forms of expertise. This is also the reason why we need an external view on such developments within criminology. In line with the critique that we formulated in section four we will aim to demonstrate that knowledge can become operative in ways that often are not captured by a power/knowledge frame. Indeed, in this case it is about how victims are depicted, how assumptions are fed, how new expectations are being raised and, ultimately, about how we see and redefine ourselves through our actions and processes of knowledge production and dissemination.

An external view on restorative justice research

'Can Mediation Be Therapeutic for Crime Victims?' This is the title of a recent research article which was published by the *Canadian Journal of Criminology and Criminal Justice*. In the paper Wemmers and Cyr (2005) explore to what extent restorative justice may help the 'healing process' of victims. They use 'therapeutic jurisprudence' as a framework to study a group of crime victims who participated in a victim-offender mediation programme in a large city in Quebec. The researchers explore themes such as victims' fear; whether participation in the programme helped them to put the event behind them; whether they benefited from the meeting; whether they judged the process to be fair; whether they were satisfied with the process followed in their case. The results discussed in the article lead them, after considering the limitations of the study, to the conclusion that procedural justice facilitates 'healing' and that mediation has contributed to the victims' well-being.

This article is one recent example of how victims' needs start to enter the restorative justice research agenda in new – therapeutically imagined – ways (for other examples and more extensive treatment, see Daems 2010). It inscribes itself in a new generation of empirical research on restorative justice where measuring positive effects on victims' well-being starts to occupy a central role. In early evaluation studies the satisfaction rate ('To what extent are participants in a restorative programme satisfied with the experience?') was already commonly used to measure the success of restorative interventions. But now we seem to be witnessing a qualitative shift: notions such as 'healing', 'closure', 'therapeutic effects', 'emotional restoration', 'reducing the sense of alienation' and so forth, point to something different, that is, restorative justice, in these recent reformulations, is no longer merely about making or keeping all participants satisfied (that is, a consumer logic), but also, and increasingly, about making victims feel better (that is, a therapeutical logic).

This stream in restorative justice research is directed at measuring positive 'victim effects': it is being underpinned by a new kind of consequentialism that strives towards 'healing victims'. The 'good consequences' that are supposed to follow from such interventions are closure, emotional restoration, trauma recovery, reducing post-traumatic stress symptoms, and so forth. In recent restorative justice research victimization is perceived to be a traumatizing event and it is hoped that the mediation or restorative justice conference, which is imagined as a therapeutic intervention, helps victims recover from their stressful experience. 'Healing victims' is being substituted for the, these days somewhat less fashionable, 'rehabilitating offenders'. This is also what Cesoni and Rechtman (2005) suggest when they identify 'psychological restoration' as a new function of punishment: like a therapy, the penal process and sanction is directed at 'reconstruction', that is, it aims at recovering victims from the psychological consequences of criminal victimization.

When criminal justice interventions are aiming at such 'good consequences' then this also might impact upon the expectations being raised towards the offender *as victimizer*. Consider, for example, the following reasons that Wemmers and Cyr (2005) presented for why victims felt less positive about their participation in a mediation programme:

> "(...) one victim did report feeling more fearful, and this was because the offender did not regret his or her behaviour and the victim felt that her or she could offend again"

> "Most victims said that they felt better with respect to their victimization after the meeting with the offender (...), but two said they felt worse. In both cases, the reason given by victims was the offender's refusal to take responsibility for his or her actions"

> "When victims suffered re-victimization, they attributed this to the offender who had failed to take responsibility for his or her actions" (Wemmers & Cyr 2005: 537, 538 & 540).

The conclusion that might be drawn from this (that is, if such a therapeutic orientation towards victims is perceived to be desirable – which seems to be a settled question for both researchers) is that, in order to enhance the well-being of victims, offenders should regret their behaviour and take responsibility for their actions. The same holds true for the importance that has been attributed to the role of apology. In *Repair or Revenge* Strang (2002: 18-23) emphasized the 'victims' need for apology' and in another recent study it was used as a criterion to measure the success of restorative conferencing: "The criterion here is whether RJ conferences result in more apologies" (Sherman *et al.* 2005: 373). This implies that victims' well-being comes, at least in part, to depend upon action taken by the offender: indeed, this research suggests that without an apology there is less chance of recovery.

To argue that criminal justice systems should heal victims, that they should strive towards certain mental health effects, is to assume that there is 'something' to heal, that is, that victims are all damaged or traumatised in one way or another. After her review of some victimological research Strang concluded the following: "All these research findings indicate *the universality of the trauma of victimization* and the high levels of dissatisfaction regarding the usual treatment victims receive at the hands of the criminal justice system" (Strang 2002: 19, my italics). After citing data from the British Crime Survey on fear of crime; various pieces of research that document victims' need for emotional support; evidence that victimization leads to 'adverse mental health outcomes'; and studies that have found that victims of property and violent crimes suffer problems which include 'severe and persistent psychosomatic symptoms and impairment in social functioning', Angel concludes, on the very first page of her study, that "(…) there is a large body of international research that illustrates *the enormity of the problem*" (Angel 2005: 1, my italics). This conclusion, then, forms the starting point for her study whether restorative justice can contribute to solving this 'enormous problem'. For Angel victims of crime, by definition, suffer from emotional problems and seem to be in need of professional help. Seen from this perspective, those who refused to participate in the experiment, then, are likely to be in denial and probably are even *more* in need for help than the others:

> "Roughly 45% of victims approached to participate in the Parent Study refused to do so, despite having a willing offender. By the nature of avoidant responses inherent to PTSD, it is quite possible that those most affected by PTSS and PTSD would decline to participate" (Angel 2005: 87).

The possibility that these victims did not feel the 'need' to participate in the programme; that in the meantime things may have happened to them which gave their lives a positive turn; that their victimization was only a minor event in their life-course; that PTSS did not dominate the victim's account of his suffering; that the natural healing process had made them recover; that they received sufficient non-professional support from their social network are not being mentioned as potential explanations. In particular the latter is strikingly absent throughout the whole research: somewhat paradoxically, the only event 'social' in nature being included in the study is the 'treatment', that is, the restorative justice conference where victims are expected to be supported by figures from their social network. Family, relatives, friends, neighbours, and so forth only come into the picture *for a couple of hours*, that is, when they play their role in the experiment, but they then magically disappear during the many months that pass between the victimization and the follow-up interview.

Like with those earlier pathologizing assumptions about offenders it is important to interrogate such assumptions. Indeed, such a general assumption of victims being 'emotionally damaged' may be neither true, nor very appealing for the persons labeled in that way. Sebba argues that "(…) many – indeed, apparently most – victimizations are overcome within a relatively short period" (Sebba 2000: 60). Fattah emphasizes the need to study the differential impact of victimization and the differential needs of crime victims: "The indisputable fact that crime victims constitute a highly diverse and heterogeneous group means that the impact of victimization and the consequences of the victimizing event will be extremely different from one victim group to another, and from one individual victim to the other" (Fattah 1999: 193; see also Fattah 2006: 93-95, 97-99). Moreover, Fattah highlights how the 'amplification of the negative effects of victimization' and the 'pathologizing of the normal reactions it evokes' leads to the creation of "(...) a specific pattern of suffering that almost forces them to feel and behave in a certain manner. Victims feel compelled to conform to this pattern of suffering because otherwise they might not be, or be seen as, normal or typical victims" (Fattah 1999: 196)[1]. Fattah offered a telling illustration that deserves to be quoted at length:

> "Let me share with you the story of a 25-year-old woman from Nova Scotia, Canada, who as a child had been a victim of incest and who last month was denied custody of her 5-year-old son, allegedly because she has not received psychological therapy to deal with her childhood victimization. The woman's words as she was interviewed by the Canadian press (...) are very telling. They illustrate what I mean when saying that we force victims into specific patterns of suffering, inculcating in their minds that they cannot cope on their own, and that their recovery hinges on getting the appropriate psychological or psychiatric treatment. Here is what the victim said:

> 'They are classifying me as this person who can't get anywhere in life because this happened, that no one can overcome something that terrible. But they don't know me. I didn't give up on life because this happened to me. It made me the person I am now.'

---

[1] Fattah also used the term 'self fulfilling prophecy' in this respect: "Telling victims of incest, rape, sexual assault, or other types of victimization that the effects are disastrous, nefarious, too serious, too traumatic, long-lasting, etc., and telling them that they cannot cope on their own without the help of psychiatrists, psychologists, sex therapists, social workers, and so forth, can easily become a self-fulfilling prophecy. It can delay the process of natural healing as well as the process of self-recovery" (Fattah 1999: 197). In his critique of the uses of PTSD Summerfield made a similar comment: "Collectively held beliefs about particular negative experiences are not just potent influences but carry an element of self fulfilling prophecy; individuals will largely organise what they feel, say, do, and expect to fit prevailing expectations and categories" (Summerfield 2001: 96).

> Then she added:
> 'I don't believe I need help, Okay? Not at the present time. May-
> be when I am 50, it might bother me, or even when I am 29. But
> right now my life is going in a positive direction, and it's not
> something that even affects me'" (Fattah 1999: 196-197).

Three years after his keynote address at the IXth International Symposium on Victimology where Fattah raised the above-mentioned worries about such developments, he predicted the 'demise of victim therapy' in the 'not too distant future'. Fattah added that the "(…) natural healing powers of the human psyche that are being interfered with, and hindered by, professional therapies, are bound to reaffirm themselves" (Fattah 2000: 41-42). In the light of our discussion in this section this prediction may have turned out to be too premature. Moreover, the focus on 'victim therapy' in the strict sense obfuscates how also criminal justice responses may get 'therapeutized' and, in their wake, lead to the implicit adoption and promotion of assumptions about victims being emotionally damaged (Cesoni & Rechtman 2005). In this sense it is, for example, remarkable how the restorative justice literature in recent years has become oriented towards researching 'victim effects' and advocating it as an attractive option for victim recovery. Indeed, such a victim-oriented 'therapeutization' of restorative justice seems to be highly incompatible with some of its core values such as active participation and reciprocal communication.

It should be clear that the particular depiction of victims of crime and their needs, have an impact upon how we respond to criminal victimization. Indeed, even though, as we argued earlier, that assumption overgeneralizes the impact of victimization and fails to differentiate between individual victims and groups of victims, it is, nevertheless, a powerful one that resonates with more wide-ranging preoccupations with mental health issues (cfr supra). One particular implication is that the image of the traumatised victim engenders new expectations towards their victimizers: the kind of person we expect offenders to be or become is not merely a law-abiding, industrious human being but also a being that has the ability to emphatize with the suffering of others and that is emotionally adequate himself. Indeed, what Wemmers and Cyr perceived to be particularly problematic in view of the therapeutic value of mediation was that offenders were not taking responsibility for their actions or did not regret what they had done to the victim. When Strang and others highlight the need for an apology from the offender to further recovery, then it is, again, the emotional skills of offenders that are being problematized.

Whether such offenders will reoffend is here (at least as long as there is no risk for revictimization of 'their' victim), to a certain extent, besides the point: offenders rather 'fail' when they lack the vocabulary and skills to move themselves into the position of their victims and, as such, may hamper the recovery of their victim (Daems & Robert 2006). When such expectations are prevalent, then also here (like in the case of Fattah's normal or typical victims who need to conform to a 'specific pattern of suffering', see above) there is a risk that a specific pattern of behaving and feeling comes to be established: the normal or typical victimizers, then, are those who produce the right set of emotions and make the expected gestures and moves. In a society preoccupied with emotional well-being, those offenders who are also victimizers may need to display not only conformity to the law but also an emotional conformity towards the victim. Raising such expectations towards offenders, then, also tells us a great deal about ourselves:

> "Expectations are raised because 'we' want 'them' to become like us. In pointing to what 'we' perceive to be inadequate in 'them', we define, by means of our expectations, what 'adequate' is. Law abiding citizens not only have to be able to make the 'right' decisions but are also required to have adequate emotional skills that enable them to forecast the harmful consequences of potential lawbreaking behaviour and that prevent them from harming one's fellow citizen" (Daems & Robert 2006: 269).

In other words, the particular ways in which we respond to criminal victimization not only tend to impact upon those victimizers, but also upon ourselves: in the process of holding out certain expectations towards offenders of crime we are defining and redefining ourselves.

Conclusion

In 2003 John Braithwaite wrote an essay in *Theoretical Criminology* with the provocative title: 'What's wrong with the sociology of punishment?' His paper was an original contribution to the debate that followed in the wake of the publication of David Garland's *The Culture of Control*. According to Braithwaite Garland's analysis focuses exclusively on societal choices whether and how to punish instead of choices whether to regulate by punishment or by a range of other strategies. Garland's focus, so Braithwaite argued, should have been regulation, not punishment. Because Garland puts punishment at the centre of his narrative his 'big picture' has a number of important gaps (such as business and white collar crime) and he creates a (false) impression that punishment is the central topic of regulation – which it arguably is not. According to Braithwaite Garland therefore remains trapped in a 'punishment of the poor' project:

> "a history of the present that traces a genealogy of punishment only through its criminal justice branches might offer inferior insights to a genealogy of regulation that opens our eyes to the ways business regulatory and criminal justice branches of the genealogy intertwine" (Braithwaite 2003: 23-24).

In this chapter we aimed to develop another critique: thinking about the uses of criminological knowledge often remains trapped in a Foucauldian power/ knowledge framework. As a result we tend to miss important aspects of how criminology impacts in ways which are, at times, unrelated to control. We have aimed to illustrate this by briefly discussing some recent research on restorative justice. As we argued in the introduction to this chapter, questions that tend to escape the strait-jacket of FAQ are often uncomfortable ones. Moreover, we realize that our reflection aims to bend back on an area of research that Braithwaite is most familiar with: after all, he is one of the key figures in the global restorative justice movement. And yet, we are also quite confident that Braithwaite will welcome such outsiders' observations on an area of research and a field of practice that he is so closely involved with. Indeed, Braithwaite himself has, at times, functioned as an outsider, as we illustrated in section two. Moreover, one of the reasons why his career is being celebrated in this book is the example that he has given to us all of how we can travel back and forth between the centre and the periphery of criminology. We can only hope that John Braithwaite will either take away our worries, or take them on board when he moves back to the heart of criminology.

References:

Angel, C.M. (2005). *Crime Victims Meet Their Offenders. Testing the Impact of Restorative Justice Conferences on Victims' Post-Traumatic Stress Symptoms*. University of Pennsylvania: Unpublished Ph.D. Dissertation in Nursing and Criminology.

Bracken, P.J., Giller, J.E. & Summerfield, D. (1995). Psychological responses to war and atrocity: The limitations of current concepts. *Social Science & Medicine*, 40(8), 1073-1082.

Braithwaite, J. (1989). *Crime, shame and reintegration*. Cambridge: Cambridge University Press.

Braithwaite, J. (2003). What's Wrong with the Sociology of Punishment? *Theoretical Criminology*, 7(1), 5-28.

Cesoni, M.L. & Rechtman, R. (2005). La 'réparation psychologique' de la victime: une nouvelle fonction de la peine? *Revue de droit pénal et de criminologie*, 85(2), 158-178.

Christie, N. (1977). Conflicts as property, *British Journal of Criminology*, 1-15

Christie, N. (1997). Four blocks against insight: notes on the oversocialization of criminologists. *Theoretical Criminology*, 1(1), 13-23.

Cohen, S. (1988). *Against Criminology*, New Brunswick: Transaction Publishers.

Cohen, S. (1991). Alternatives to punishment – The abolitionist case. *Israel Law Review*. 25, 729-739.

Cohen, S. (1997). Conference Life: The Rough Guide. *The American Sociologist*, 69-84.

Daems, T. (2005). Repeat victimisation and the study of social control. *International Journal of the Sociology of Law*, 33(2), 85-100.

Daems, T. (2008). *Making Sense of Penal Change*. Oxford: Oxford University Press.

Daems, T. (2010). Death of a Metaphor? Healing Victims and Restorative Justice. In: Shoham, S.G., Kett, M. & Knepper, P. (eds.), *International Handbook of Victimology*. Boca Raton: CRC Press, Taylor & Francis Group, 491-510.

Daems, T. & Robert, L. (2006). Victims, knowledge(s) and prisons: victims entering the Belgian prison system. *European Journal of Crime, Criminal Law and Criminal Justice*, 14(3), 256-270.

Fassin, D. & Rechtman, R. (2007). *L'Empire du traumatisme. Enquête sur la condition de victime*. Paris: Éditions Flammarion.

Fattah, E.A. (1999). From a Handful of Dollars to Tea and Sympathy: The Sad History of Victim Assistance. In: Van Dijk, J.J.M., Kaam, R.G.H., Wemmers, J.-A.M. (eds.), *Caring for Crime Victims. Selected Proceedings of the Ninth International Symposium on Victimology. Amsterdam, August 25-29, 1997*. Monsey: Criminal Justice Press, 187-206.

Fattah, E.A. (2000). Victimology: Past, Present and Future. *Criminologie*, 33(1), 17-46.

Fattah, E.A. (2006). Le sentiment d'insécurité et la victimisation criminelle dans une perspective de victimologie comparée. In: Born, M., Kéfer, F. & Lemaître, A. (eds.), *Une criminologie de la tradition à l'innovation. En hommage à Georges Kellens*. Brussels: De Boeck & Larcier, 89-106.

Foucault, M. (1977). *Discipline and Punish. The Birth of the Prison*. London: Allen Lane.

Foucault, M. (1980). Prison Talk. In: C. Gordon (ed.), *Power/Knowledge. Selected Interviews and Other Writings 1972-1977*, New York: Harvester Wheatsheaf, 37-54.

Furedi, F. (2004) *Therapy Culture. Cultivating Vulnerability in an Uncertain Age*. London: Routledge.

Galassi, S. (2004). *Kriminologie im Deutschen Kaiserreich. Geschichte einer gebrochenen Verwissenschaftlichung*. Stuttgart: Franz Steiner Verlag.

Garland, D. (1985). Politics and Policy in Criminological Discourse: A Study of Tendentious Reasoning and Rhetoric. *International Journal of the Sociology of Law*, 13, 1-33.

Garland, D. (1997). The Punitive Society: Penology, Criminology and the History of the Present. *Edinburgh Law Review*, 1, 180-199.

Garland, D. (2001). *The Culture of Control. Crime and Social Order in Contemporary Society*. Oxford: Oxford University Press.

Garland, D. (2008). Disciplining Criminology? *International Annals of Criminology - Annales internationales de criminologie*, 46 (1/2), 19-37.

Hulsman, L.H.C. (1980). *Reader 4a. Strafrecht. Studiejaar 1979/80*. Rotterdam: Erasmus Universiteit Rotterdam.

Hulsman, L.H.C. (1986). Critical criminology and the concept of crime. *Contemporary Crises*, 10, 63-80.

Lyon, D. (2003). *Surveillance after September 11*. Cambridge: Polity Press.

Nolan, J.L. Jr. (1998). *The Therapeutic State. Justifying Government at Century's End*. New York: New York University Press.

Pupavac, V. (2002). Pathologizing Populations and Colonizing Minds: International Psychosocial Programs in Kosovo. *Alternatives*, 27(4), 489-511.

Pupavac, V. (2004). International Therapeutic Peace in Bosnia. *Social & Legal Studies*, 13(3), 377-401.

Rechtman, R. (2002). Être victime: généalogie d'une condition clinique. *L'Évolution Psychiatrique*, 67, 775-795.

Rechtman, R. (2004). The rebirth of PTSD: the rise of a new paradigm in psychiatry. *Social Psychiatry and Psychiatric Epidemiology*, 39, 913-915.

Rusche, G. & Kirchheimer, O. (1939/1968). *Punishment and Social Structure*. New York: Russell and Russell.

Scott, W.J. (1990). PTSD in DSM-III: A Case in the Politics of Diagnosis and Disease. *Social Problems*, 37(3), 294-310.

Sebba, L. (2000). The Individualization of the Victim: From Positivism to Postmodernism. In: Crawford, A. & Goodey, J. (eds.), *Integrating a Victim Perspective within Criminal Justice. International Debates.* Aldershot: Ashgate, 55-76.

Sherman L.W., Strang, H., Angel, C., Woods, D., Barnes, G.C., Bennett, S. & Inkpen, N. (2005). Effects of face-to-face restorative justice on victims of crime in four randomized, controlled trials. *Journal of Experimental Criminology*, 1(4), 367-395.

Strang, H. (2002). *Repair or Revenge. Victims and Restorative Justice.* Oxford: Oxford University Press.

Summerfield, D. (1999). A critique of seven assumptions behind psychological trauma programmes in war-affected areas. *Social Science & Medicine*, 48, 1449-1462.

Summerfield, D. (2001). The invention of post-traumatic stress disorder and the social usefulness of a psychiatric category. *British Medical Journal*, 322, 95-98.

Wemmers, J.-A. & Cyr, K. (2005). Can Mediation Be Therapeutic for Crime Victims? An Evaluation of Victims' Experiences in Mediation with Young Offenders. *Canadian Journal of Criminology and Criminal Justice*, 47, 527-544.

BRAITHWAITE, CRIMINOLOGY AND THE DEBATE ON PUBLIC SOCIAL SCIENCE

IAN LOADER AND RICHARD SPARKS[1]

"The essential need, in other words, is the improvement of the methods and conditions of debate, discussion and persuasion.
That is *the* problem of the public."

(Dewey 1927: 208; emphasis in original)

Introduction

We are involved in an extended project – or rather, though it still feels somehow immodest to put it in this way, a linked series of projects potentially extending over a number of years - aimed at re-thinking the character and scope of contemporary social science work on crime, justice and public policy.[2] Part of this work is concerned with contextual questions and with tracing historical connections amongst ideas and the policy outcomes that they have supported. This is pretty much what we had in mind in earlier work in advocating an *historical-sociological* approach to crime policy (Loader and Sparks 2004).

Clearly this means that criminology itself, and the many associated discourses and trades with which it connects, is an object of interest and investigation for us. However, as we hope to make clear here and elsewhere, we do not see these concerns as merely introspective, or as justifying an attitude of self-

---

[1]   Ian Loader is Professor of Criminology and Director of the Centre for Criminology, University of Oxford. Richard Sparks is Professor of Criminology, University of Edinburgh and a co-director of the Scottish Centre for Crime and Justice Research. As our job titles suggest we each now find ourselves bearing certain responsibilities for the development of a research group. In this regard the analysis we undertake here, and the larger enterprise to which it relates, is not for us an abstract or idle pursuit. It goes to questions that engage the objectives and activities of our working lives.

[2]   Sections of this chapter are based on a paper delivered to the European Society of Criminology Conference, Bologna, September 2007 as 'A successful failure?: on the predicaments of European criminology today'. This was an initial outing of a much larger joint project, the first substantial outcome of which is published as a book entitled *Public Criminology?* (Routledge, 2010).

absorption and withdrawal. We are well aware that the 'sociology of social science' does not on the face of it sound a very promising enterprise from a practical point of view. Yet to the extent that our project involves turning some of the tools of social scientific analysis onto the processes of knowledge-production and circulation themselves, we want to use any insights we can offer precisely to reflect upon questions of the uses, applications and possibilities of criminological knowledge (and conversely the circumstances in which it is disregarded or countermanded by political interests, prior moral convictions and so on). In other words, if we are serious about *applying* knowledge or *influencing* policy we had better strive to achieve some clarity about what these terms can feasibly mean, how to recognize those processes in action, and what the ethical, intellectual and political implications of such claims may be.

We are therefore interested in the roles, stances and commitments of those who have participated in such activities – their intellectual, personal and professional identities, so to speak, and the varieties of social networks and relationships in which they have been engaged. We want to make such issues the object of serious (historical and, in principle, comparative) investigation and in so doing to ask pertinent questions about 'influence', 'relevance' and so on. We want to know something about what people mean by these sorts of terms, and about their social conditions of existence, not just about how to acquire more of the assets (profile, prestige or whatever) that they appear to promise.

In the first part of that project, and a bit later in this paper, we look across from 'within' criminology, whatever this may mean, towards a nearby debate in sociology stimulated by Michael Burawoy's several important contributions on 'public sociology'.[3] Burawoy's position, as we briefly outline below, has stimulated a substantial critical response and has engendered both enthusiastic support from many and trenchant rebuttal from others. In this sense, it has provoked a relatively intense period of discussion and appraisal on the failings and achievements, problems and prospects of sociology, even if that discussion has been largely confined within the academy (and overwhelmingly North

---

[3] The second and third parts of the project involve, next, some more serious contemporary history, in particular of ideas and engagements in post-war British social science and public policy; and, finally, should we ever get there, to think afresh about certain criminological problems and questions from the perspective of their implied relations with political theories.

American in focus and assumptions).[4] As we go on to explain below, there may be specific reasons why scholars of crime and punishment (the people doing what we will continue to call criminology, for want both of any better term and of any compelling reason not to do so) find themselves in need of some tools and resources for similar reappraisal. Clearly, criminology has not been without its own factionalisms, schisms and outbreaks of culture warfare down the years. Moreover, and more particularly, criminology currently faces – at least in some places in which it is practised – certain allegations of lack of usefulness and capacity. These are in some respects similar to the conditions that precipitated Burawoy's intervention, if not indeed really just instances of the same issues. Similarly, many criminologists -like social scientists working in a range of fields- are understandably attracted by the idea of a more pronounced and involved public role, and thus expressly drawn to Burawoy's terminology. For these reasons the question of 'public sociology' is also of direct and active interest for criminology.

In our view it is instructive to think about these questions through the prism of the work of John Braithwaite, for several reasons. First of all Braithwaite has himself made a characteristically incisive and non-obvious contribution to the 'public sociology' discussion, he is thus part of the critical response with which we need to come to terms. From him, for example, we borrow the term 'public social science', rather than either public sociology or public criminology (Braithwaite 2005). As Braithwaite has indicated on more than one occasion he takes a distinctly sceptical view of disciplines in general and the disciplinary formation 'criminology' in particular (Braithwaite 2000, 2003). By common agreement Braithwaite has contributed greatly to criminology but has clearly never been bound by it and perhaps not even particularly attached to it. Braithwaite's commitment to a trans-disciplinary social science seeking transformative discoveries is one of the most striking features of his *modus operandi*. Finally, Braithwaite is a remarkable example, perhaps, in our area of interest, a uniquely successful example, of someone who has managed to

---

[4]   On this point Loïc Wacquant comments with characteristic trenchancy: "I prefer the term *civic* to *public* sociology (which has recently come into fashion among American sociologists), since such sociology seeks to bridge the divide between instrumental and reflexive knowledge and to speak simultaneously to both academic and general audiences --albeit in different harmonics. The dichotomous opposition between public and professional sociology is a peculiarity of the US intellectual field, expressive of the political isolation and social impotence of American academics, that does not travel well outside of the Anglo-American sphere and does not adequately capture the positional predicament of university sociologists in America either." (Wacquant 2009).

sustain a distinguished scholarly research career in continual dialogue with practice communities and civil society groups. If anyone is in a position to speak to (or at any rate whose work we can use to help find a route through) the seeming fixities of the academic-practice division of labour, or the adequacy of the kinds of taxonomy we are offered vis a vis 'public' and other sociologies (see below) it would be he.

For reasons we go on to explain in the next section the need for reflection on just these issues –the roles, possibilities and promise of social science in respect of public problems and purposes on one hand; the obstacles and exclusions, pitfalls and seductions of various forms of engagement on the other– seems pronounced just now.

The predicaments of criminology today

Consider the following two reflections on the state of, and prospects for, criminology uttered by two past Presidents of the American Society of Criminology in the course of their Presidential addresses:

> "The strength of our numbers and the core characteristics of our discipline position us to be one of the central disciplines of the twenty-first century."
>
> (Zahn 1999: 1)

> "Several signs suggest that this influence [on criminal justice policy and practice] is weakening and that our research and analysis may be becoming less relevant to the practices and problems of the system than they used to be."
>
> (Petersilia 1990: 1)

It is no doubt true that Presidential addresses invite these kinds of dramatic diagnoses and prognoses – whether optimistic or gloomy. Yet these contrasting assessments of the condition of contemporary criminology are of wider importance because they capture the two sides of what has of late assumed the status of orthodoxy – in the mainstream of Anglo-American criminology at least. Criminologists are doing more and more, and in some respects (at least technical ones) they are doing it better and better, yet to less and less effect in terms of the formation and priorities of public policy. In a reaction essay in *Criminology and Public Policy*, James Austin robustly summarises this orthodox position: "Despite the annual publication of hundreds of peer-reviewed articles and textbooks proudly displayed at our annual conventions, policy makers are paying little if any attention to us" (Austin 2003: 557). Cullen (2004: 2) similarly notes that "most criminological research, including mine, is ignored".[5]

The contemporary situation of criminology is sometimes described as paradoxical – the paradox being one of 'successful failure'. On the one hand, criminology appears to be booming. We have in recent years been witness to new courses, more jobs, more students, new journals, more and larger conferences, new professional associations, the creation and awarding of prizes. By all these standard measures the field is in excellent health. On the other hand, this has coincided with, maybe even been an integral part of, the rising prominence of crime within the mundane culture and political programmes of a number of societies, and the increasing drift towards more punitive solutions to crime and more intrusive approaches to security issues that is evident today. Viewed in this light, the recent success and future directions of criminology seem more uncertain. This diagnosis is perhaps articulated in its most pronounced form in the United States, with the United Kingdom echoing it quite closely,[6] and with elements of similarity and divergence in evidence across Europe.

Different diagnoses typically accompany this observation. One of these detects a fall in *demand* for criminological knowledge within the institutions of government. As criminology has grown and its research output and hence potential to inform public policy has mushroomed, so government has turned away. It has become less willing to commission criminological enquiry into crime problems, drawn more towards a more compliant research consultancy market and increasingly pursues policy agendas that dance to the tune of other voices – typically those pressed by the media, or gleaned from focus groups or opinion polls. There has, in the process, been a weakening of the shared assumptions about what government can and should properly do to govern crime in a democratic society around which criminological practitioners and government officials were once able, from their respective institutional

---

[5]   Cullen however then goes on to recount a tale, about the survival and resilience of the concept of rehabilitation which for him stands as an exception to the generally understood rule.

[6]   It may be more precise here to say that the debate in England and Wales has echoed the American one quite closely. The Scottish debate, though clearly marked by similar concerns, is not identical (see further McAra, 2008).

locations, to make common cause, coupled with the propensity of government to encroach – in the name of public safety – upon the values and institutions that liberal criminologists continue to hold dear.

A second, contrasting, analysis pinpoints a shortfall in the *supply* of quality criminological goods. The growth of criminology, it is said, has been accompanied by criminologists turning away from government. The result is an inward-looking profession absorbed in a world of arcane journals and conferences; a field talking to itself which lacks the research skills that can assist in solving contemporary crime problems and whose practitioners are unwilling or unable to speak to audiences beyond the academy. The more criminology has grown, in other words, the more it has fractured into self-referential specialisms that have lost their essential connection with the public concerns that they ostensibly address, and which provide criminology with its *raison d'être*. This in fact is the diagnosis that Petersilia offers. Criminologists, she claims, have become insular and insulated, habituated by their training and reward structures to publish in journals read only by other criminologists and refrain from disseminating their work in wider settings (Petersilia 1990: 8-9). But the argument has also been pressed by others – both by those working inside government (Wiles 2002) and by academic criminologists urging their colleagues to subject ill-informed, punitive penal agendas to public challenge (Currie 2007). In an interview with one of the present authors, a senior figure in British criminology spoke of a 'mutual moving apart' between criminology and government and of criminological practitioners who 'have no idea how to talk to policy-makers'. He continued:

> "Where is the oppositional political criminology? Where are the researchers who are actually challenging government policy on the basis of evidence and research? Where is that kind of criminology in this country? I don't know about you, but I don't see that debate."

These, then, are some of the elements of what has become a common and influential interpretation of the condition of contemporary Anglo-American criminology. But how accurate an assessment is it?

We would be wise to pause before accepting, without qualification, this characterization of the situation of criminology today and the explanations that accompany it. We might ask here whether, as a matter of empirical fact, criminology is failing, or being reduced to a marginal place within a shrill, populist penal culture. Are there not plenty of examples – to put a neutral gloss on it – of criminology remaining closely connected with and influential upon crime control and penal policy – think of situational crime prevention, or problem-oriented policing, or preventative interventions focused on risk and protective factors, or restorative justice programmes; or even of criminological concepts having altered the vocabulary within which contemporary societies think about crime and its control – moral panics, hot-spots, police culture? One might note, further, that national and sub-national governments, criminal justice institutions and many forms of media continue to seek out – if not always to heed – criminological wisdom and advice. Some of these – notably the police – have demonstrably become closer to, rather than more remote from, criminology in the last two decades, at least in the United Kingdom (the case we know best and to which we will refer most frequently).[7] And one can record that processes of responsibilization, pluralization and globalization have resulted in a proliferation of *both* the range and number of agencies involved in the governance of crime (to include, *inter alia*, public bodies like transport or housing authorities, private corporations, national and trans-national NGOs, and the European Union) *and* the demand for, and opportunities to promote, criminological knowledge and expertise. The empirical picture is to say the least uneven, an unevenness which complicates any one-dimensional tale about criminology's waning influence and marginality (Young 2003; Zedner 2003).

Yet even were one to accept that today criminology exercises little direct influence on policy in a world of spiralling imprisonment, actuarial justice and encroachments upon individual liberty - an insecure world which is in

---

[7] Consider here the example of the Scottish Institute for Policing Research (http://www.sipr. ac.uk/), which describes itself as: 'a strategic collaboration between twelve of Scotland's universities and the Association of Chief Police Officers in Scotland, funded by the Scottish Funding Council, offering a range of opportunities for conducting relevant, applicable research to help the police meet the challenges of the 21st century and for achieving international excellence for policing research in Scotland.' The Institute's programme of work includes new Ph.D. studentships, conferences, workshops and new educational opportunities for serving police officers. In Wales the Universities' Police Science Institute (http://www.upsi.org.uk/) makes a similar claim: 'UPSI was established to enhance the quantity and quality of research evidence for policing, and to use results from academic studies to improve police policy, practice and training. The research conducted by UPSI spans theoretical, methodological and applied themes. Our work in the following areas has been particularly influential at national and international levels.' One could no doubt cite similar examples throughout Europe and elsewhere, though these are two recent and notable cases. Indeed it would be interesting to conduct an institutional, comparative inquiry, but this is beyond the scope of this chapter.

Jonathan Simon's (2007) phrase 'governed through crime' - why call this failure? Has criminology really 'failed' simply because some political rulers or criminal justice actors choose to pursue crime and penal policies in ignorance – wilful or otherwise - of its hard-earned lessons? Surely this is akin to blaming the toxicologists rather than the shop's managers for an outbreak of food poisoning among a supermarket's customers.

The task of criminology, one might argue is - recalling Edwin Sutherland's still hard-to-beat definition of the field – to generate knowledge about 'the processes of making laws, of breaking laws, and of reacting toward the breaking of laws' (Sutherland *et al.* 1992: 3), not to be expert in getting others to accept or act upon that knowledge – a task that anyway lies very much beyond criminologists' individual or collective control. Why, moreover, should we assume or accept that governmental bodies are the principal audience for criminological research? One might equally retort that the hallmark of scientific enquiry is that its exponents interact first and foremost with one another in search of answers to internally generated intellectual puzzles, not externally set agendas. Alternatively, one could note that there are a very wide array of practitioner communities and social movements that call upon, interact with and indeed often produce criminological knowledge. To presuppose the centrality of 'The Government' as audience, as some critics seem to do, is to disregard some important aspects of the conditions under which knowledge of crime and justice is actually generated and circulated.

Conversely, one cannot simply assume that because criminology appears in good health when measured by the yardsticks described above (more conferences, students, journals etc.) that this necessarily makes it a 'success'. One judges the field by the quality of its efforts to explain and understand those aspects of the social world that are brought under its gaze, not by totting up the number of outputs produced. The total may, after all, be largely an effect of 'massive overproduction and loss of quality control' (Abbott 2007: 206).

We need, moreover, to recognize the parochialism, or at least specificity, of the idea of successful failure. This depiction emerges from – and makes at least some sense in – the US and England and Wales, societies where a criminology that was once closer to centres of power, and once "cautioned the nation about underlying social needs and problems" (Skolnick 1994: 2), has seen its expansion inside universities coincide with the decline of a receptive constituency within government who shared criminology's liberal commitments and were minded to call upon its practitioners for counsel and advice.[8] It is a process one of us has elsewhere described as the fall of the 'Platonic guardians' (of whom criminologists counted as associate members); one which underpins and helps account for the tendency of some US and English criminologists to bemoan – *but rarely explain* – their loss of influence and the alleged irrationality of contemporary political responses to crime (e.g., Blumstein 1992; Radzinowicz 1999; see, further, Loader 2006). We might thus acknowledge that the successful failure paradox illuminates some aspects of crime control in those political cultures which have been most radically reshaped by neo-liberalism since the 1970s and where penal policy has become more punitive in substance and populist in style, as well as pinpointing certain of the tensions and dilemmas that this creates for criminology (cf. Wacquant, 2009). It remains an interesting and open question how just this situation looks in other jurisdictions across Europe – in the newly democratized states in Central and Eastern Europe, in nations not all of whose political cultures and social relations have been similarly or equally colonized by crime; or in states with strong constitutional traditions and civil – rather than common - law institutions and legal cultures and so on.

We cannot enlarge further on the paradoxes or curiosities of contemporary criminology here but refer to our recent book (Loader and Sparks 2010). For now we hope to have done enough to show why the paradox of successful failure only partially illuminates, and in some ways obscures, the condition of contemporary criminology. Yet as this paradox dissolves, or we at least leave it behind, a series of real dilemmas moves into view – dilemmas that the idea of successful failure in part helped to highlight, and which do indeed confront criminologists today, however much they vary in their intensity and precise form across different jurisdictional settings. These dilemmas have several salient elements. They are, first, very far from being novel or of recent vintage – the issue of how to reconcile the competing claims of autonomy and engagement, knowledge production and social relevance raises questions about the relationship between social science and politics that are as old as the social sciences themselves and, indeed, severely exercised their founders. They are, secondly, open to being addressed in a number of ways – most often through the medium of personal – and always potentially narcissistic

---

[8]   The symbolic high watermarks of this criminological influence remain, in the US, the 1967 report of The President's Commission on Law Enforcement and the Administration of Justice on *The Challenge of Crime in a Free Society*, and, in England and Wales, the 1959 Home Office White Paper on *Penal Practice in a Changing Society* (Home Office 1959).

- reflection and stance-taking (whether public or private) among individual scholars, or by means of an – all too often ahistorical - journey into and through the philosophy of social science. Nor, it should be added thirdly, are they amenable to any easy, definitive resolution.

None of this is sufficient though to gainsay their contemporary relevance and importance which, in our view, cannot be wished away. The issues of what topics criminologists work on, how they work on them, the forms of knowledge they strive to produce, the audiences they envisage for their work, the intersections between that work and government, the positions criminologists assume and interventions they make in wider public controversies about crime, punishment, security and the like – the question, in short, of *what is criminology for?*; these are conundrums that have long vexed – and ought properly to vex - those who embark on the social analysis of crime and punishment. Yet they arise for consideration today in a world radically altered from that in which the field of criminology was formed in the late 19th century, or the one in which it helped produce and configure penal-welfare states during the middle decades of the 20th. It is a world in which security questions have become paramount; a world where crime and punishment tend – albeit unevenly – to assume more prominent and contentious places in the political cultures and quotidian relations of contemporary societies; a world dominated and reconfigured by the dizzying technological change and a '24/7' media culture; a world in which the 'local' and 'global' interact in ways that have potentially profound ramifications for crime and its control. These are times, in short, that call into doubt the answers that might once have been adequately given to the question of criminology's public purpose; that bring this question sharply back into focus and delimit in new ways the plausible answers that one may give to it. For all these reasons, the whole issue seems, to our minds at least, to stand pressingly in need of more sustained historical enquiry and sociological analysis than it has tended thus far to receive.

We outline the contours of just such an enquiry into criminology's public purposes and relations to the surrounding political culture in the final section. First, however, we briefly consider some ways in which these issues have latterly been discussed in a neighbouring area of inquiry and the implications of that discussion for criminology.

Whether we will continue to call this activity of reflection on crime, social regulation and social justice *criminology* at the end of this process is another question. Some observers are quite hostile to criminology as a disciplinary-institutional formation and take its entrenchment to constitute a constraint on our ways of re-imagining crime and justice – we discuss a couple of versions of this view below. Others, of whom we take Braithwaite to be one, are largely indifferent to it and believe there are many more important questions to attend to. We are cautiously friendly to criminology, though this essay and all our work in this area represent, among other things, a determination to defend pluralism in the ways in which it is defined and practised. Retaining the label, for at least some purposes, and even being committed to practising *as a criminologist* under some definition of the term, must not in our view be used as a pretext for failing to inquire into that field's institutional conditions of existence, or failing to register the fuzziness and contingency of its boundaries, or indeed envisaging some future conditions in which it might cease to be useful or relevant. In particular, as we go on to argue, we think there are good reasons for being suspicious of attempts to flourish disciplinary identifications as means of imposing closure or of channelling out topics or perspectives that challenge whatever concerns or priorities the subject is assumed to happen to have just now.

The 'public sociology' debate and its lessons

Criminologists are not alone among social scientists in worrying over and debating the shape, relevance and uses of their subject in complex times. In the adjacent field of sociology a now extensive and vigorous debate has sprung up in a strikingly short time on these very points, circulating around the theme of `public sociology'. The intensity of that debate seems clearly to indicate that for many practising sociologists – and possibly, as we shall go on to outline in relation to criminology, for some of the `users' (or former or would-be users) of their work – these concerns strike close to the heart of the purposes and scope of the subject. Moreover, given the starting points of that debate, not to mention the obvious conceptual and historical propinquity between sociology and criminology anyway, this is arguably not merely an *analogous* discussion (from which we might learn something by inference or extrapolation) but rather a nearby instance of the *same* problem.[9]

---

[9] This is not to suggest, however, that the main articulations of the issue are without problems, still less that they can simply be imported uncritically into criminological argument as the 'solution' to current difficulties. We are in need of conceptual refreshment here, not easy answers.

In a series of trenchant and influential statements Michael Burawoy has sought to re-focus sociologists' attention on the question of the public role or purposes of the discipline.[10] Burawoy claims that there are four principal styles or registers of sociological writing and research. He terms these *professional*, *policy*, *critical* and *public* sociologies. Burawoy insists that he wishes to *distinguish* these rather than to *separate* them: they are for him mutually constitutive and necessary dimensions of the sociological enterprise, existing in creative and dynamic tension, rather than distinct and self-contained entities. They may be differentiated in various ways however – by their underlying epistemological premises, for example; by the degree of their claims to autonomy from external agendas or sponsorship; by their implied or express audiences or interlocutors; and hence, perhaps most significantly, by their commitment to engage with a public sphere that exceeds the boundaries of the academy as such.

Thus *policy sociology* is sociology in the service of goals or questions defined by a client; providing solutions to problems presented to us or legitimate solutions already arrived at. *Professional sociology* signifies the multiple and intersecting programmes of research as classically understood within the academy – its good health is the *sine qua non* for either policy or public sociology to take place effectively. *Critical sociology* is concerned with an examination of foundations, critical commentary on professional or policy activity. Critical sociology is "the conscience of professional sociology just as public sociology is the conscience of policy sociology". *Public* sociology brings sociology into conversation with a public, understood as people who are themselves involved in conversations – a dialogic relation, a discussion involving values or goals that are not automatically shared by both sides … an activity in/of civil society, collapsing neither into state nor market. It envisages sociology itself as an intermediary institution. Burawoy maps the relations between the four modes as follows:

---

[10]   One such intervention took the form of his presidential address to the ASA in 2004 – a public, as well as a disciplinary, venue for a reflection on the publicness of sociology. For concision we focus on this utterance here, although the position has been further elaborated since.

	Professional	**Policy**
Knowledge	Theoretical/empirical	Concrete
Legitimacy	Scientific norms	Effectiveness
Accountability	Peers	Clients/patrons
Pathology	Self-referentiality	Servility
Politics	Professional self-interest	Policy intervention
	Critical	**Public**
Knowledge	Foundational	Communicative
Legitimacy	Moral vision	Relevance
Accountability	Critical intellectuals	Designated publics
Pathology	Dogmatism	Faddishness
Politics	Internal debate	Public dialogue

Source: Burawoy, M. (2004) 'Public Sociologies', *Social Forces*, 82/4: 1603-18.

Burawoy is well aware that reflection on the public purposes of sociological writing recurs throughout the history of the subject. It is present in Durkheim's late reflections on moral education and civic responsibility, in Weber's famous essays on science and politics as vocations, in Mills's impassioned criticisms of the pathological temptations of grand theory and abstracted empiricism, in Gouldner's and Becker's exchanges about side-taking, underdog sympathies, everywhere in feminist sociology and social theory and so on before and since. Burawoy is deeply versed in these traditions and alludes to each of them at various points (Burawoy 2006, 2007). However, he begins this discussion from a strikingly similar vantage point to our own reflection on the paradoxes of criminology, namely that in his view, the institutional embeddedness and scale of sociology now, is not matched either by a coherent account of the public roles and purposes of the subject nor by any marked success in shaping the contours of public discourse or policy. Indeed, he argues, by comparison with the earlier comparators, sociologists today are relatively absent from the main channels of societal conversation and opinion-formation. Thus the scale, scope and institutional weight of the activity exist in an inverse relation to its public effectivity, and it is this frailty that Burawoy urges sociologists to address.

Burawoy's intervention has struck a major chord and incited weighty criticism as well as plaudits. It is undoubtedly interesting and apposite to consider why this has been the case although we have space to note only a few of the responses here. The debate on public sociology has now occasioned special issues of major journals on both sides of the Atlantic, stimulated symposia and been recorded in a number of books (e.g. Blau and Smith, 2007, Clawson et al., 2006). Amongst the lines of criticism of most interest to us are those that riposte by defending the claims of *professional* sociology from what they take to be a dilution of its claims to rigour, autonomy and intellectual ambition. To sacrifice these to the immediacies of relevance and engagement (and so perhaps of what is generally known in the British context as `knowledge transfer'?) is to undermine the legitimacy of the enterprise itself and so to undercut whatever authority sociology enjoys *qua* sociology. Thus, for example, Tittle identifies four major problems with public sociology: (i) it involves false assumptions, such as the idea that 'social justice' is a clear, value-free concept, and that sociological knowledge is certain and definite; (ii) it endangers the limited legitimacy that sociology has, by shifting sociologists' identities from generators of knowledge to advocates of positions; (iii) it is incompatible with good professional sociology, because publics are rarely interested in 'truth', but rather in finding help for their existing views; (iv) it is incompatible with the idea of participatory democracy, because it values the sociologist as more than equal in discussing current affairs.

This debate has now also begun to register in criminology.[11] This response has had a number of features that we find problematic:

i   it has tended by and large to take the form of a somewhat uncritical importation of Burawoy's typology and cognate effort to fit criminology into it;

ii several contributors have somewhat uncritically championed the analogous idea of a 'public criminology' – as if it appeals as an 'off-the-shelf' means of affirming that there *is* something important and relevant about criminology (without this meaning working primarily for government);

iii both the debate in sociology and its importation into criminology have a 'bricks without straw' quality – endless iterations of personal identification with (or distancing from) the public sociology/criminology idea.

---

[11]   For example in a special issue of *Theoretical Criminology*, in Gordon Hughes's book *The Politics of Crime and Community* (2007); in the blog of that name by Christopher Uggen, and so on.

We need to learn from these moves, some of which now look to us rather mistaken. We might also notice, *en passant*, that the intensity with which the public purposes of sociology and now criminology have recently been debated has not prevented that debate from becoming rather inward-looking and of interest mainly or only to professional sociologists and criminologists. This seems a standing, albeit somewhat ironic, danger. But we must avoid too the opposite error of introducing Burawoy and then making no analytic use of his analysis – as if this were all 'for information only'. So our preliminary task is to examine how Burawoy's typology/analysis can illuminate, indeed shed new light on, various arguments within criminology (if indeed the notion of criminology having an inside or outside any longer makes sense) about its role and purpose.

Braithwaite (and Ericson) on public social science

Here is where Braithwaite comes back in. This is not only in the obvious sense that his own career exemplifies as clearly as any other we can think of the ability to cleave equally fervently to the requirements of social scientific professionalism and of public engagement for purposes of changing the world. Those commitments may have acutely differing demands but they do not, in this case, necessarily involve some sort of irreconcilable conflict or even a division of labour such that an individual can specialize, so to speak, in only one of them. John Braithwaite has over several decades, in the course of enquiries into white-collar and corporate crime, regulatory compliance, restorative justice and (now) peace-building, generated a body of work that combines explanatory and normative theory, makes concrete the implications for crime and justice of republican political thought, clearly specifies the political and policy implications of his research, and worked with social movements and activists without compromising either scholarly rigour or intellectual curiosity. It seems important to note that Braithwaite's work in restorative justice has developed in an acknowledged association with the commitments and values of a social movement; that this has over time stimulated an increasingly sophisticated body of theoretical work, both normative and explanatory in character; that it has in the course of these developments migrated from a somewhat peripheral to an increasingly central position in both scientific and policy discussion; and that Braithwaite's own practice has betrayed no sense of contradiction between the strength of the commitments underlying this project and a willingness to subject the empirical claims for effects of restorative interventions to rigorous testing and investigation, including the use of randomized experimental trials. The view implicit in this vision of research practice is that criminological research is at its most illuminating, and has most to offer to public life, when it operates across these domains.

Seen in this light we would suggest that it is not altogether surprising that some of the most challenging and constructive critical responses to Burawoy have come from commentators whose work has been centrally concerned with questions of crime and justice. For now we can discuss only two of these, namely those by Braithwaite himself and by the late Richard Ericson. Certainly, perhaps with some minor adjustment (and possibly some apology), one could readily find criminological candidates for occupancy of a customized version of each of Burawoy's boxes. Nevertheless, some of these more criminologically-oriented commentators are especially sceptical of the very divisions on which Burawoy's model relies. Why might this be? Is it that criminology already knows that it has at most a thematic rather than a strictly disciplinary or theoretical unity? Are its practitioners therefore already relatively comfortable with a degree of pluralism, and receptive to the view that both normative and explanatory questions, legal and jurisprudential issues as well as empirical inquiry, matters of political and cultural interpretation and critique as well as more tightly controlled observations and evaluations are all legitimately amongst its concerns?

Thus, in a characteristically urbane and subtle intervention, Ericson argues that the four-way division that Burawoy proposes is inherently unsatisfactory. He is still unhappy with any suggestion that any individual thinker stands only in one of the four spaces at any given time. For him, Burawoy forgets that *all* sociology is, or ought to be, 'critical'. This has two aspects. First, 'being critical is a core element of professionalism':

> "Critical inquiry is what scientists, indeed all academics, do as professionals, challenging assumptions, theories, methods, findings and implications of research. As Burawoy himself recognizes, research entering into policy and public contexts only has credibility if this scientific ethos of critical challenge and independence remains at the core of professionalism." (Ericson, 2005: 366)

Sociology is also inherently critical in its "refusal to accept social structures, institutions, processes, and relations in the terms in which they are conventionally presented", and that its "violations of commonsense" and attempts to "educate through irony" typically lose their impact once translated into the communication formats and criteria of relevance operated by other social institutions, whether they be government, the police, courtrooms or the media (Ericson 2005: 366-67; see also Beck 2005: 337). Ericson thus acknowledges the disjunctures, distortions and hesitations that may arise for social scientists as they attempt to bring their findings, insights and propositions into the public domain, where other rules and communicative styles operate. On the other hand Ericson concurs with Giddens's estimation of the cultural salience of the social sciences.[12] Their direct and instant impact on policy may often be slight, but this is a secondary matter compared with their constitutive role in modern societies:

> "As Giddens (1990: 16) remarks, 'the practical impact of social science and sociological theories is enormous, and sociological concepts and findings are constitutively involved in what modernity is'. Sociology originated, developed and sustained legitimacy as part of the modern, liberal, social imaginary of producing data on populations that contribute to governmental programmes of security, wellbeing, prosperity and self-govern-ance (Taylor 2004). As such it has always been integral to policy, defined simply as principled courses of action. Moreover, as analysts of principled courses of action, sociologists cannot escape making choices among preferred principles and thereby contribute to policy."

In Ericson's view, the condition to which Burawoy's intervention responds, however fractious, remains a phoney war. The boundaries between Burawoy's quadrants are chronically mutually permeable. In this sense, just as 'professional' or 'policy' work may be 'critical', it is somewhat dubious to select only certain styles of work as 'public':

> "All sociology entails public knowledge. There is no such thing as 'private' sociology in the sense of self-referential practitioners who do not actively seek to publicize their ideas and research. Sociologists publicize their ideas and research in myriad in-stitutional contexts involving various audiences and different

---

[12] Giddens's views on this matter derive from his distinctive views on the nature of social sci-entific knowledge, and in particular the argument that these are characterized by a 'double hermeneutic' in virtue of which 'lay' and 'technical' concepts have a two-way relationship. On this view "the concepts of the social sciences are not produced about an independ-ently constituted subject-matter, which continues regardless of what these concepts are. The 'findings' of the social sciences very often enter constitutively into the world they describe." (Giddens 1987: 20)

media. The media include classrooms at various levels of education (schools, colleges, universities, graduate schools), textbooks, research monographs, journals, government reports, mass media (television, radio, newspapers, magazines), and websites that can also be used to intersect with each of the above media." (Ericson, 2005: 369)

Ericson's assertion of the plural and inherently public character of sociological work nevertheless rests upon a robust defence of unfettered academic inquiry.[13] On this view the losses in translation involved in many encounters between social scientists and media, and the incursions upon autonomy that, he says, result from striving for 'relevance' and funding can be heavy prices to pay.

Braithwaite (2005) also trenchantly challenges the thrust of Burawoy's project to the extent that this appears to be concerned to salvage, or to revitalize, *a discipline*. Like Ericson, Braithwaite presents a strong argument for intellectual pluralism. His more radical charge is that Burawoy has launched an outmoded bid to rescue and revitalize sociology in particular (in whichever of its four registers) and established disciplinary formations in general. This Braithwaite thinks is misplaced. He argues instead that the complexities of our times demand a public *social science* (rather than sociology *or* criminology *or* whatever), one that engages in theory-driven attempts to assemble whatever trans-disciplinary resources are required to address the intellectual projects and practical activities at hand. We require, in other words, a social science with "more tents and fewer buildings" (Braithwaite 2005: 351). For this reason public social science is significant in a way that public, or any other, sociology – still less criminology – just is not.

---

[13] This is not to suggest that all academics fulfil their public roles with equal commitment or distinction. The argument that all social science is public threatens to reduce to circularity and drain the notion of 'the public' of much meaning. Conversely the notion of 'public' this or that can become near-redundant when a whole scholarly life really is committed to public purposes. Thus, as Neil Walker remarked in his address at the memorial service for Professor Sir Neil McCormick in Edinburgh in April 2009: "Neil also excelled as what we might term a public intellectual. I use the term with some hesitation, not just because Neil might have balked at its over-stylization - at its hint of self-importance, but more tellingly because he would have found the adjective 'public' simply redundant. For Neil, in order to be true to one's vocation as an intellectual one must be prepared to 'go public', so to speak. One had to engage with the issues of the day; one had a duty to develop and disseminate new ideas for dealing with these issues; and one was required to express healthy scepticism before all conventional wisdom, whatever its source."

Re-thinking the 'failure' and promise of criminology

Why have we thought it worthwhile to revisit the public sociology debate here in this fashion? What are its implications for the study of crime and justice today? And what does this have to do with the evaluation of the 'successful failure' motif in competing accounts of contemporary criminology. Rather more pressingly, what does this mean for considerations of the future character, roles and social value of social science work in this field, broadly considered?

For us there are three main sets of reasons why these things matter. Firstly, we began (and we will shortly return to this in conclusion) by discussing certain estimations of the condition or 'shape' of criminology. Many of these, we have suggested, have been oddly negative in character. Exponents of the 'successful failure' paradox may well have grounds for regretting the limited reach of criminological scholarship into public policy or everyday public consciousness, but the chiding tone of their allegations can be disabling and disempowering. If we are going to undertake the evaluation of criminology's 'track-record' over the last half-century or more, let us do that in a way that is as comprehensive, fair-minded, contextually rich and historically rigorous as we can manage. Most of the narratives of failure and decline lack these features. Their jadedness assorts oddly with their disguised partisanship: if only more of this had been done in this way or that way we would not be in this fix now. Like all mid-life crises this one mingles regret and recrimination, accentuates the negative, takes from the past only what it prefers and fails utterly to focus on the future. There must be better ways of discussing the history of the subject's present condition than this.

Secondly, we draw from the critical discussion of the public sociology debate, and especially from the interventions of Ericson and Braithwaite, a vigorous defence of theoretical, methodological, disciplinary and political pluralism. Here then is the very beginning of a sketch of our own interpretation of the disciplinary dilemma, so to speak, of criminology today. There appear to be several recurring tendencies within the field which have in common the effect of closing down discussion, or of sealing off different discussions from one another. We might usefully discuss three of these here, all of which we find somewhat worrying:

i) *Hyper-specialisation/Balkanization*. By this we mean the effort to handle the fragmentation and diversity (in aims, methods, questions posed, disciplines drawn on, commitments expressed, audiences supposed) that has accompanied the expansion of criminology by in various ways institutionalizing (and thereby cementing) the salient differences of focus and purpose. Much of this is just the harmless consequence of the enlarged scale of the enterprise, and represents a pragmatic adaptation to its diversity. Presumably no one intends that the organization of the American Society of Criminology, for example, through its (perhaps all too aptly named) 'Divisions' – of critical criminology, women, people of colour, international criminology etc (and perhaps soon of public criminology?) – should be *divisive*. There is nothing unusual or very surprising in the proliferation of discrete study groups, conferences and journals dedicated to subfields and specialist interests. Much of this is innocent enough - necessary and even valuable to the production and discussion of knowledge. The pathology, to borrow Burawoy's term, would lie in succumbing to the risk of 'fixing' these divisions as if they were natural; of either leaving intact and under-scrutinized the 'core' that does not need its own division, or denying the field has any core concerns or agreed upon knowledge base at all; of positing these sub-fields as incommensurable, hermetically-sealed clusters of activity that have nothing to learn from each other and which participants in the field one can do little more that choose between. The result: a world of criminologies passing like ships in the night – in ways, perhaps, that undermine its legitimacy in the wider world and hence its public purpose?

ii) *Legislative utterance/declaratory acts*. By this we mean the act of declaring that criminology *must* from here on do this or that if it is to be more useful or regain the legitimacy and social value that it might once have possessed. We might cite three contemporary cases in point:

   a) *criminology must inform Government*: Paul Wiles, whose intervention has already been mentioned, has argued that criminology can serve the public good best – and perhaps only – by reconnecting itself to the policy agendas and dilemmas of elected government and being able to contribute to evidence-based policy-making. Wiles finds – at least British – criminology unevenly equipped for this task.

   b) *criminology must produce robust, testable knowledge for purposes of directing interventions*: Lawrence Sherman (2006, and elsewhere) in his vigorous and articulate championing of experimental method in criminology argues that the subject will be useful primarily – and perhaps only - by subjecting programmes and knowledge claims to randomised control trials (the 'gold standard') and through rigorous meta-reviews of evaluations.

   c) *criminology must resist*: conversely, Reece Walters argues that at this point in its development, and in the face of the present condition of the political and policy fields criminology can only generate relevant, insightful and challenging work when it resists the pull of government, commits itself to a critique of neo-liberal rationalities and produces emancipatory knowledge. For Walters to participate in Government-sponsored research in the United Kingdom at present 'is to endorse a biased agenda that omits topics of national and global concern in favour of regulating the poor and the powerless (2008: 20). Instead: "If criminology is to survive or is to make any sense it must embrace diverse knowledges of resistance; in my view, criminology must be a knowledge of resistance. (2008: 22)

For all their substantive differences as to what criminologists are supposed to do, these moves in our view have rather more in common than their proponents would readily admit. They are in our view 'legislative statements' in very much the sense intended by Bauman (1987). By "making authoritative statements which arbitrate in controversies of opinions" (Bauman 1987: 4), and by seeking to bring the conduct of others into line with their preferred vision of the field such statements tend to resort to caricature in the description of criminology's history and current situation. Secondly there is advocacy of one, privileged road to valid or useful knowledge and social utility; and there is a closely related assumption that there is nothing of great value to be learned from certain other ways of defining and studying criminology's subject matter.

It is an ambition of our project to find a way into and through the question of criminology's public purpose that avoids such resort to legislative reason. Of course one of the easiest ways of falsifying these restrictive utterances about conditions of utility is that certain people – John Braithwaite is one such – have successfully done all three. Amongst the points to which Richard Ericson (2005) objected in Burawoy's account is precisely the suggestion that, notwithstanding the *systemic* linkages between the four sociologies, each of us tends only to stand in one box at a time.

iii) *Dissolution/abandonment*. This too has been a recurrent tendency within the field. It has taken the form of either the claim that criminology is politically and intellectually compromised by its founding reliance on ideological, state-based categories (notably, crime) and needs to be replaced by enquiry organized around alternative vocabularies (e.g., problematic situations, conflicts, ordering, regulation); or it has made the claim that criminology's incoherence and instability as a field of enquiry can only be solved by collapsing it back into one of its 'parent' disciplines (usually sociology, increasingly today psychology). Sometimes the arguments advanced here are subtle, sophisticated and still worthy of attention, sometimes they are less so. Certainly some of their advocates have made a powerful case for subsuming criminology within the wider study of social and legal regulation (Braithwaite, 2000), even if they are more kindly disposed to the notion of 'criminology' as such (Shearing, 1990). Let us for the moment focus on two other contemporary instances of the argument for abandonment:

a) *crime science*: Ronald Clarke has argued that criminology (especially in its more sociological orientations) has diverted attention away from potentially useful points of intervention to prevent or reduce crime and towards things that cannot easily be altered. It has also tended to give itself up to speculation and idle theorizing. It may therefore be approaching the point at which it needs to be *superseded by* a new field of crime science. This might draw upon those things it finds useful from criminology, but only as one of many contributing resources. The new focus: using science to find and test practical ways of cutting crime. Crime science, it is argued, is more 'outcome focused' than criminology – a science that is prepared to "sacrifice some scholarly rigour in favour of timeliness and relevance" (Clarke 2004: 60). Whereas some people associated with the 'crime science' position anticipate a relationship of 'cohabitation' and 'fruitful dialogue' (Smith and Tilley 2005: xviii) others – notably Clarke himself – seem less accommodating. Clarke depicts criminology as social reformist, anti-business in outlook, habitually aligned with the 'criminal underdog' rather than the victim, and incapable of addressing real-life problems. Should it collectively fail to adapt its mission, theories and methodologies in ways which make it "more directly relevant to crime control", Clarke argues, "universities may begin to create new departments of crime science, instead of building departments of criminology" (Clarke 2004: 55).

b) *zemiology*: In the view of Paddy Hillyard and colleagues (2004) criminology (and the criminal law categories and associated notions of intent and responsibility around which it is organized) focuses attention on a small range of social harms, typically not those that have the greatest individual and social cost. The task then is to develop a critique of the discursive power of criminology to frame how societies think about selective responses to social harm, including the harms produced by the over-application of criminal law itself. Criminology ultimately must be *dissolved* in favour of the sociology of harm and social policies that respond more comprehensively and rationally to harms in all their forms. Criminology cannot help much here because it is 'infected with individually based analysis, explanation and "remedy"' (Hillyard et al. 2004b: 270). Notwithstanding the resistance to such approaches that have been generated from within the field itself, and the sheer diversity of contemporary criminological work, "criminology cannot entirely escape such discursive practices because of what it is, where it was born, and how it has been constructed" (ibid.).

What is wrong with all this? Why indeed should we think there is *anything* wrong with it when we too feel a strong intuitive sympathy for many of the objectives that the zemiologists hold dear? What's wrong, we think, is (again) in both cases the reductionist caricature that is created of the field that is being left behind and to shore-up the critique using some arbitrary definition of what criminology is or isn't, or can or cannot be (criminology does and can only do this . . .).

We would like to suggest instead that criminology's 'vice' as a field – the impurity of its disciplinary lineage and fuzziness of its boundaries - can also be envisaged as, and made into, a virtue.

Towards an historical hermeneutics of criminology

Let us remind ourselves why we have embarked on this critical review of some of the recurring tendencies found within the criminological field. The constitution of criminological institutions, and their programmes of research and teaching cannot be done without answers being expressly or by default given to questions about the work criminologists can and should do, the questions it seems especially important to answer, the methods selected to address them, and the audiences towards which such work is addressed. They depend on decisions being taken about what students need to be taught and whether there is, or should be, any 'core' to a criminology curriculum. And they involve determinations of what is meant by 'relevance' or 'usefulness' or 'significance' when applied to work in the field, as well as decisions about whether, and if so how, to use criminological knowledge to seek to influence policy formation or to contribute to wider public debates about crime and punishment. These questions, we have suggested, press upon the field with renewed force, and in a revised light, in the early years of the 21st century.

When these questions are subject to explicit treatment in public they characteristically take the form of personal or autobiographical reflections on a career or body of work – not least because they are a staple of the inaugural lecture. This often results in their treatment being episodic and unsystematic, conducted with reference to limited empirical data, too often assuming the form of idiosyncratic, necessarily partial acts of self-justification – the 'from-a-distance' consideration by the individual scholar of his or her takes on what criminology is for and why it matters. It is perhaps this that has underpinned the accusation that such reflection on, and scrutiny of, the criminological field by its practitioners can be little more than 'navel-gazing'; an activity that may be of self-indulgent interest to its participants, but which is scarcely likely to excite anyone else. As we have said, the public sociology debate is currently at risk of repeating, in a concentrated burst, this catalogue of errors. The result is that we have a series of family quarrels and internal disputes but these stand "very far from a genuine reflexive sociology" (Bourdieu 2000: 33).

We propose to try to break with this way of doing things. We believe that what is required instead, attempted less often, but likely to prove of much greater value is a research effort that makes the field of criminology itself the focus of sociological enquiry. This, importantly, means treating the worlds of knowledge production and policy formation of which criminologists are, or wish to be, insiders, practitioners and participants as proper objects of enquiry over which one must acquire some critical, reflexive distance. For only by doing so can we hope to shed new light on, and come to see in new ways, practices that we can too easily fail to understand because we (think we) know them too well. To achieve this we would need – as the late French sociologist Pierre Bourdieu (1984) nicely put it – 'exoticize the domestic'; find ways, that is, of rupturing an "initial intimacy with modes of life and thought which remain opaque because they are too familiar" (see also Loader and Sparks, 2004).

We are well aware, of course, that our position on this and Braithwaite's differ somewhat, even though he appears as a somewhat exemplary character in this story. Braithwaite's position bears an at least passing similarity to that of the zemiologists but he is, famously, relaxed about criminology and its future. At the risk of vulgarizing the position, we might say that for Braithwaite the important thing is that scholarship addresses the world we inhabit now, rather than resting content with an organization of knowledge that reflects the conditions that have existed in the recent or more distant past when fields or disciplines emerged. Disciplines, even ones that have played some important role hitherto, may reach a point of obsolescence and so become impediments to insight (Braithwaite, 2000). If practices and institutions of social ordering and regulation change in really significant ways so that the concentration of powers of criminalization and punishment in the hands of nation-states are exposed as just one mode of regulation among others then it is time to move on. To retain an exclusive focus on criminal justice, as the symbolic focus of the capacities of the *soi-disant* sovereign state, becomes a misdirection of effort. It is to mistake an historical echo (albeit one that may still carry much resonance and emotive charge, not to mention its powers to arrest, deprive, detain and incarcerate) for the contemporary reality, let alone the scope of future possibilities.

We are continually astonished by the bravery and creativity of John Braithwaite's scholarly work and practical interventions. We can think of few lives of civic scholarship that we find more admirable. Yet we are not quite prepared to accept this version of history, or its depiction of the present and near future, if only because we think that the history itself has as yet only been very partially explored. If we are to avoid simply producing a more sophisticated version of the 'successful failure' trope which, we have argued, is inherently problematic as a platform from which to address the future, then a few of us need to stay behind long enough to pick up some of the threads and scraps and see what we can weave out of them.

This is why we have rehearsed (perhaps even laboured) the argument for an historical sociology – or, more accurately, an historical hermeneutics - of criminological knowledge from at least the mid 20th century to the present. Our argument is that if we collectively were more genuinely curious about the pasts and presents of criminology then we would pursue work with something like the following purposes, methodological orientations and rationale:

i) *Purposes*. The project would take as its substantive aim a systematic investigation into, and reconsideration of, the diverse roles, responsibilities and commitments of criminological scholars and researchers since the mid 20th-century. What have criminologists characteristically done and not done? What positions have they taken up – on the levels of theory, research, expertise and intervention – vis-à-vis the great controversies of their periods? What positions of proximity, distance or opposition have they occupied in respect of the centre of decision-making or influence, or in the intervention and reform of practices and institutions? What does that tell us about what may be possible or not possible now?

ii) *Methodological orientations*. The project would draw upon key programmatic statements and other criminological writings of recent decades, as well data such as extended biographical interviews (similar to those that one of the authors has conducted with leading criminologists, government officials and penal reformers who were active in the 1960s and 1970s in the UK: see Loader 2006). By mobilizing the orientation and methods of historical hermeneutics and the interpretive analysis of ideology and ideologies associated with writers such as Quentin Skinner, John Dunn and Michael Freeden (Tully 1989; Skinner 2002; Freeden 1996; Dunn 2000), it would offer a creative reconstruction of the dispositions and outlooks that scholars and other actors have adopted towards the world of politics, public policy and penal reform during the latter half of the 20th century; consider their relation to the institutional, social and political conditions under which these commitments and affiliations arose, appeared plausible and unravelled; and address the effects these competing perspectives have had on the contours and aspirations of criminology and the world beyond. A vital commitment of this methodology is to give the 'best possible account' of the positions that have competed for influence in the academy and beyond during this period – in a bid to forestall the premature closure of contemporary possibilities and keep alive the idea that these positions may have – unexpected – things to learn from mutual dialogue with one another.

iii) *Rationale*. The rationale for conducting such an enquiry is in some measure at least historical – to improve our knowledge and understanding of the recent history of criminology, the controversies that have animated the field, the social and political conditions that have shaped the field and within which the field has sought to have, and has indeed had, effects. But our concerns are also more contemporary. For it is our belief, indeed this is the intuition that has prompted us to embark upon this enquiry, that a sociological account of the criminological field and its mutually conditioning intersection with politics and culture since the mid 20th century can offer a set of orientations for the present. It can, in particular, do what the best sociology has always done: clarify the *limits* of what is possible, and hence what *may be* possible, in this case for criminologists seeking to renew the public purpose of their field of social enquiry in the altered conditions of the early 21st century.

By way of conclusion

Part of the ambition of hermeneutic inquiry in many of its forms (historically, anthropologically, philosophically) is to do with overcoming barriers to mutual comprehension – the famous 'fusion of horizons' of which Gadamer speaks. For us this is the contribution that historical hermeneutics might offer to the future of criminology. It would serve to emphasize that criminology's public value lies in part in the very plurality of theoretical perspectives, focal concerns and methodologies that it comprises – to paraphrase Braithwaite it is already rather more like an encampment than an edifice. However, it would also attend to the range of ways it can be put to work in the service of fostering public deliberation and political discourse. Mindful of the field's tensions, it favours an attempt to foster exchange, debate and accommodation between different criminological approaches, and to highlight the costs of the tendencies towards over-specialization, legislation and abandonment that we described above. Ultimately of course the intentions of such efforts at mediation go well beyond the internal concerns of the criminological academy. They speak in favour of seeking to create institutional spaces that foster new kinds of deliberative practice and engage affected publics in imaginative ways. This, in the end, is the central issue and task that the public social science debate places before us.

References

Abbott, A. (2007) 'For Humanist Sociology', in D. Clawson, R. Zussman, J. Misra, N. Gerstel, R. Stokes, D.L. Anderton and M. Burawoy (eds.), *Public Sociology*. Berkeley: University of California Press.

Austin, J. (2003) 'Why Criminology is Irrelevant', *Criminology and Public Policy*, 2/3: 557-564.

Bauman, Z. (1987) *Legislators and Interpreters*, Oxford: Basil Blackwell.

Beck, U. (2005) 'How not to Become a Museum Piece', *British Journal of Sociology*, 56/3: 335-344.

Blau J. and Smith, K. (2006) *Public Sociologies Reader*, Lanham, MD: Rowman and Littlefield.

Blumstein, A. (1993) 'Making Rationality Relevant', *Criminology*, 31/1: 1-16.

Bourdieu, P. (1984) *Homo Academicus*, Cambridge: Polity.

Bourdieu, P. (2000) *Pascalian Meditations*, Oxford: Oxford University Press.

Braithwaite, J. (2000) 'The New Regulatory State and the Transformation of Criminology', in D. Garland and R. Sparks (eds.), *Criminology and Social Theory*, Oxford: Oxford University Press.

Braithwaite, J. (2003) 'What's Wrong with the Sociology of Punishment', *Theoretical Criminology*, 7/1: 5-28.

Braithwaite, J. (2005) 'For Public Social Science', *British Journal of Sociology*, 56/3: 345-354.

Burawoy, M. (2004) 'Public Sociologies: Contradictions, Dilemmas and Possibilities', *Social Forces*, 82: 1613-1626.

Burawoy, M. (2006) 'The Field of Sociology: Its Promise and Power', in D. Clawson, R. Zussman, J. Misra, N. Gerstel, R. Stokes, D.L. Anderton and M. Burawoy (eds.), *Public Sociology*, Berkeley: University of California Press.

Burawoy, M. (2007) 'Public sociology: Mills vs. Gramsci', Socio*logica*, 1/2007: 7-12.

Chancer, L. and E. McLaughlin (2007) 'Public Criminologies: Diverse Perspectives on Academia and Policy', *Theoretical Criminology*, 11/2: 155-173.

Clarke, R. V. (2004) 'Technology, Criminology and Crime Science', *European Journal of Criminal Policy and Research*, 10: 55-63.

Clawson, D., R. Zussman, J. Misra, N. Gerstel, R. Stokes, D.L. Anderton and M. Burawoy (eds.), *Public Sociology*, Berkeley: University of California Press.

Cullen, F. (2005) 'The Twelve People Who Saved Rehabilitation: How the Science of Criminology Made a Difference', *Criminology*, 43/1: 1-42.

Currie, E. (2007) 'Against Marginality: Arguments for a Public Criminology', *Theoretical Criminology*, 11/2: 175-190.

Dewey, J. (1927/1954) *The Public and Its Problems*, Oxford: Holt.

Dunn, J. (1990) *Interpreting Political Responsibility*. Cambridge: Polity Press.

Ericson, R. (2005) 'Publicizing Sociology', *British Journal of Sociology*, 56/3: 365-372.

Freeden, M. (1996), *Ideologies and Political Theory: A Conceptual Approach*. Oxford: Oxford University Press.

Gadamer, H-G. (2002) *Truth and Method*, trans. Joel Weinsheimer and Donald G. Marshall, 2nd revised edition, New York: Continuum.

Garland D. and R. Sparks (2000) 'Criminology, Social Theory and the Challenge of our Times', in D. Garland and R. Sparks (eds.), *Criminology and Social Theory*, Oxford University Press.

Giddens, A. (1987) *Social Theory and Modern Sociology*, Cambridge: Polity Press.

Giddens, A. (1990) *The Consequences of Modernity*, Cambridge: Polity Press.

Hillyard, P., C. Pantazis, S. Tombs and D. Gordon (eds.) (2004), *Beyond Criminology: Taking Harm Seriously*. London: Pluto Press.

Home Office (1959) *Penal Practice in a Changing Society*, London: HMSO.

Hughes, G. (2007) *The Politics of Crime and Community*. Basingstoke: Palgrave.

Laycock, G. (2005) 'Defining Crime Science', in M. J. Smith and N. Tilley (eds.), *Crime Science: New Approaches to Preventing and Detecting Crime*, Cullompton: Willan.

Loader, I. And R. Sparks (2010) *Public Criminology?: Criminological Politics in the Twenty-first Century* (Key Ideas in Criminology). London: Routledge.

Loader, I. (2006) 'Fall of the "Platonic Guardians": Liberalism, Criminology and Political Responses to Crime in England and Wales', *British Journal of Criminology* 46/4: 561-586.

Loader, I. and R. Sparks (2004) 'For an Historical Sociology of Crime Policy in England and Wales since 1968', *Critical Review of International Social and Political Philosophy*, 7/2: 5-32.

McAra, L. (2008) 'Crime, Criminology and Criminal Justice in Scotland', *European Journal of Criminology*, 5/4:481-504.

Petersilia, J. (1990) 'Policy Relevance and the Future of Criminology', *Criminology*, 29/1: 1-14.

President's Commission on Law Enforcement and Administration of Justice (1967) *The Challenge of Crime in a Free Society*, Washington: US Government Printing Office.

Radzinowicz, L. (1999) *Adventures in Criminology*, London: Routledge.

Shearing, C. (1990) 'Decriminalizing Criminology: Reflections on the Literal and Tropological Meaning of the Term', *Canadian Journal of Criminology*, April, pp. 169-78.

Sherman, L. (2005) 'The Use and Usefulness of Criminology, 1751-2005: Enlightened Justice and its Failures', *Annals of the American Academy of Political and Social Science*, 600: 115-135.

Simon, J. (2007) *Governing Through Crime: How the War on Crime Transformed American Democracy and Created a Culture of Fear*, New York: Oxford University Press.

Smith, H. J. and N. Tilley (2005) 'Introduction', in M. J. Smith and N. Tilley, eds, *Crime Science: New Approaches to Preventing and Detecting Crime*, Cullompton: Willan.

Skinner, Q. (2002) *Visions of Politics: Volume 1 – Regarding Method*, Cambridge: Cambridge University Press.

Skolnick, J. (1994) 'What not to do About Crime', *Criminology*, 33/1: 1-15.

Sutherland, E., D. Cressey and D. Luckenbill (1992) *Principles of Criminology*, 11th edition, Lanham MD; Rowman and Littlefield.

Taylor, C. (2004) *Modern Social Imaginaries*, Durham: Duke University Press.

Tittle, C. (2004) 'The Arrogance of Public Sociology', *Social Forces*, 82/4: 1639-1643.

Tully, J. (1989) *Meaning and Context: Quentin Skinner and his Critics*. Princeton: Princeton University Press.

Uggen, C. and M. Inderbitzen (2006) 'Public Criminologies', paper presented at the Annual Meetings of the American Sociological Association, Montreal. Available at: http://www.soc.umn.edu/~uggen/uggen_inderbitzin_TC2006.pdf

Wacquant, L. (2009) *Prisons of Poverty*, Minneapolis: University of Minnesota Press.

Walters, R. (2004a) *Deviant Knowledge: Criminology, Politics and Policy*. Cullompton: Willan.

Walters, R. (2008) 'Government manipulation of criminological knowledge and policies of deceit' in T. Hope and R. Walters (eds.), *Critical Thinking about the Uses of Research*, London: Centre for Crime and Justice Studies.

Ward, K. (2006) 'Geography and Public Policy: Towards Public Geographies', *Progress in Human Geography*, 30/4: 495-503.

Wiles, P. (2002) 'Criminology in the 21st Century: Public Good or Private Interest?, *Australian and New Zealand Journal of Criminology*, 35/2: 238-252.

Wiles, P. (2004) 'Policy and Sociology', *British Journal of Sociology*, 55/1: 31-34.

Young, J. (2003) 'In Praise of Dangerous Thoughts', *Punishment and Society*, 5/1: 97-107.

Zahn, M. (1999) 'Thoughts on the Future of Criminology' *Criminology*, 37/1: 1-16.

Zedner, L. (2003) 'Useful Knowledge?: Debating the Role of Criminology in Post-war Britain', in L. Zedner and A. Ashworth (eds.), *The Criminological Foundations of Penal Policy: Essays in Honour of Roger Hood*. Oxford: Oxford University Press.

WHY RESEARCH CANNOT BUT BE TRANS-DISCIPLINARY IN COMPLEX MATTERS OF ETHOS AND JUSTICE

BART PATTYN

Introduction

In their preceding chapter, Ian Loader and Richard Sparks have started an interesting discussion. Sociologists and criminologists are considering whether they should be involved in the social debate and contribute to policy-supporting research. They are wondering whether, if they do so, they will still meet the strict requirements of scientific research, and conversely, if they don't get involved, whether their research will still be relevant. The debate on the limitations of one's own scientific expertise and the conditions of claiming the right to speak as an expert is, in itself, an interesting topic for sociological research. However, there is more at stake than only the search for truth or defining the scope and limits of a methodological strategy. As Pierre Bourdieu (1988) and Michel Foucault (1971) have written (in *Homo Academicus* and *L'ordre du discours* respectively): the struggle about the right to speak as an expert also involves academic politics. As Loader and Sparks suggest, John Braithwaite does not seem very concerned about territorial delineations of disciplines. It seems irrelevant to him under which colours scientific research on urgent social problems is sailing, as long as it does sail. He obviously approaches scientific research from his commitment to a better world and does not let his social concerns be dictated by what is most convenient scientifically.

My contribution will focus on the motives behind specialisation and try to figure out how ethics can be involved in a trans-disciplinary reflection on social control, shame and reconciliation.

Expertise and the politics of specialisation

Not being a sociologist nor a criminologist, I cannot judge the disciplinary limitations of competence that operate within these fields. I do not feel qualified to do so even in my own field of ethics. To define the limitation of an expertise, one must first be sure that there actually is one. What kind of expertise a philosopher should have, is in itself a philosophical question. We all know that Socrates enjoyed making scholars confess that they knew less than they professed to know. He appears to have been an expert at questioning that, but it is not likely that this is the kind of expertise that philosophers have appealed to ever since. Nonetheless, the problems described by Loader and Sparks sound familiar within current academic philosophy and especially ethics. Some ethicists consider it their duty to get involved in social debate. They claim to be experts in corporate ethics, biomedical ethics, or environmental ethics and easily speak out on these ethical questions in public, especially if they are susceptible to the honour of those questions being asked precisely to them. Other ethicists distance themselves from any kind of popularisation and withdraw into their domain specific literature, for instance of Kant, Hegel, Habermas, or Rawls. That kind of diversity seems to be enriching, and is probably of all times. Still, there is something disturbing about the developments of recent years in the social sciences and humanities that stem from the increase in pressure to achieve. Young researchers feel more and more compelled to specialise in a particular detail of a subject, because that strategy increases their chances to publish in international journals, an aspect that they will be judged on mercilessly.

Specialisation seems self-evident when you aim for progress in the investigation of the complex reality in different domains, but as a side effect, fewer people are inclined to take into account the consequences of these specialised advances. Scientists who invest their time and energy in specialised research will by definition not look across the divide, but even people with a broad range of interests are not capable of doing something sensible with the specialised conclusions of current research. Essayists, culture critics and journalists do not have the time and means, and researchers themselves do not appear to be interested in fitting their conclusions into a broader framework and attuning it to what researchers from parallel disciplines discover. Because of specialisation, field specific jargon has differentiated even more in the past years. As a result, scientists have become unintelligible to one another, a fact that hardly seems to disturb them. In fact they have since long silently buried the illusion that the puzzle of partial research results will be put together one day. Most academics do not need to be convinced of the limited relevance of their knowledge. Out of honest scrupulousness they think it is better to be good at something they can meticulously verify, than to be uncertain about things they cannot get an overall view of. They think it is safer to master everything that can be said of a specific partial topic, than to look for larger insights that are less and less interesting to scientific journals because their quality is so hard to verify. It is not only a dutiful scrupulousness that has made scientists limit their expertise, but also a need for security. The best way to make sure you get to have an academic career is choosing a topic of which you meet the other fifty researchers at international colloquia every year. The smaller the inside group of experts who cite, evaluate, review, and congratulate each other, the higher the chances of internationally cited publications and favourable peer reviewers when applying for research funds. In those circumstances it is plainly injudicious to display an interest in social problems. Modern scientists thus know precisely more and more about less and less, and almost nothing anymore about increasingly more. Even in education itself is the interest in broad introductory visions dwindling, which means that explanatory theories sink into oblivion.

It is therefore no coincidence that the debate on the social duties of academics crops up in times like these. Without explicitly admitting it, many scientists realise that self-referential research has reached the limits of the absurd. That is why the research of John Braithwaite is refreshing. It is not primarily meant to be impressive in specialised academic circles, even though by now it has become exactly that. Braithwaite seems to focus on injustice in this world that can be prevented, wounds that have been inflicted and can be healed. Understanding and study are the means to that, and not an aim by themselves. And Braithwaite's research is exciting precisely because his ideas and theories are meaningful to many disciplines, including ethics.

The current specialisation trend has various causes and no one is able to indicate which factors explain the phenomenon most adequately: specialisation is incited by the idea that a division of labour is the best strategy for gaining more understanding in different domains of knowledge in this complex world, but specialisation also rests on the attempt of researchers to distinguish themselves. They like to define their own territory in view of academic politics. Specialisation helps to rule out incalculable factors and it meets the need to find cover from the outside world among the likeminded. Apart from its practical advantages, specialisation rests on the implicit belief that there are essential principles that can be studied on their own within a specific discipline without mentioning all kind of related phenomena that are studied in other disciplines. Economic factors are said to be independent of legal factors and ethical factors of psychological factors: all these field-specific principles are handled as if they exist on their own. Anyone who thinks this through will realise that this implicit presupposition is problematic, but usually this is not dwelt upon and the illusion is kept up that reality is conditioned by nicely separated principles that can be studied independently.

The unreflective presupposition that reality answers to separated principles seems to go back on an old tradition associated with Plato and Aristotle, characterised by the belief that reality has developed from certain underlying ideas or essences. These principles are invariable, like mathematical concepts, and they do not need what is different from themselves to mean what they mean. One does not have to take their context into account; one doesn't have to know anything about their history or the customs within which they surface or the symbols that express them. After all, those principles would be entirely independent of contingent developments. A philosopher who can picture eternal invariable principles gains essential knowledge without having to take stock of the culture, history, or social situation within which that knowledge can be meaningful. Within philosophy itself, this paradigm has been overturned. Since the mid-twentieth century, philosophers have made it clear that what we see as meaningful is the result of cultural, social, and historical processes that have influenced a broad evolving collective system of meaning. While the metaphysicians could cherish the illusion of being able to ignore all sciences because philosophical knowledge is independent from what is different from itself, the modern philosopher realises that to understand what is going on, he has to know the contingent context. This belief is disturbing for the delineation of philosophy. It means that instead of reflecting on what is essentially philosophical and unassailable to economic, anthropological, cultural, sociological, psychological and linguistic factors, philosophers now have to turn towards the world and take into account all these elements that are not part of their field. That is why I am uncertain about what kind of expertise a philosopher can pretend to have.

Although this reasoning is consistent and most philosophers have left the old metaphysical paradigm behind, there are still a lot of unreasoned thoughts on the meaning of principles that would independently organise reality: psychological principles could be studied on their own, as you can research economics without taking into account the history of sociology. All these domain-specific features of reality would answer to different autonomous principles. Therefore each introduction to a discipline starts with a delineating definition of the subject and few scholars question this kind of practice. So the conception I have described regarding the metaphysical tradition still survives within other disciplines, among them ethics.

Indeed, ethics is often perceived as a specific discipline that is concerned with purely ethical principles that should be carefully distinguished from other principles, for instance legal, criminological, sociological, or anthropological principles. Most handbooks on ethics mention that these ethical principles could be derived from ethical theories. An ethical theory seems to be a structure of propositions, which, like a scientific theory, provides a framework of beliefs. The initial beliefs on which the framework is based are often taken as intuitions with an intellectual power of arriving at abstract truths. The various existing ethical theories are founded on very different basic intuitions. Some are founded on the intuition that "actions are right in proportion as they tend to promote happiness, wrong as they tend to produce the reverse of happiness" (Mill 2002), others are founded on the intuition that "I ought never to act except in such a way that I could also will that my maxim should become a universal law" (Kant 1997). Such theories are often used as a tool to determine whether a certain act should be seen as a moral obligation; whether the person involved is reproachable or whether his behaviour can be justified. Ethical theories present themselves as adequate instruments for the bookkeeping of someone's moral debts. It is as if these theories can help you to calculate the purity of your soul as a finite anticipation of a divine perfect judgement. Stating what is right and wrong in this context is often seen as the expertise of ethicists. It functions as a special form of knowledge based on principles that are definitely different from economic, sociological, or psychological research.

This practice is deceptive (Williams 1993). It can only pretend to be relevant because it does not take our personal identity and our world seriously. It starts from a false representation of reality. We simply do not live in an world that answers to pure ethical principles. Social practices, historical conceptions, legal regulations, and moral habits are strongly interrelated. The most an ethical theory can do is cultivating the narcissist awareness of having fulfilled every requirement of a implausible justificatory assumption. Someone who sees this kind of comfort as the ultimate objective of an ethical reflection displays an immoral indifference to many things that people care about in real life (Frankfurt 1988). People worry about very different things than the purity of their own soul. They care about their work, children, or partner, for instance. They are interested in the well-being of their community, in art, or in history. Most of these moral projects are outside the scope of what ethical theories try to cover. If you want to study them, you need to be involved in history, psychology and sociology; you need to understand how things of importance appear within a particular cultural context and how people within that particular context have made differences between what seems valuable, virtuous, right, or good.

The reasons why abstract ethical theories seem to make sense goes back to the attractiveness of the intuitions they are built on. It is obviously sensible to verify whether a decision has painful consequences and it may be useful to investigate whether others would make the same decision in similar situations. But the idea that the generalisation of intuitions like these and the complex derivations that follow from them can lend stability to a theory to determine, *a priori*, and from an Archimedean point in the universe, whether a certain behaviour is morally acceptable, is doubtful. The narrowing down of ethics to a reflection on justification theories has always been and still is unwholesome.

In this context, the conclusion is that to have impact an ethical reflection should not be limited to calculations based on nicely separated so-called ethical principles but should investigate what is going on in reality. This implies that one should take into account diverse factors that are not solely ethical or philosophical. One should also consider people's worldviews and the diverse projects they want to realise within specific historical, legal and economic contexts. There are many historical, legal, psychological, economic, and cultural factors to take into account. Probably the same applies to other disciplines: whenever someone reflects on law or criminology he cannot limit himself to the purely legal or criminological. There are always other things involved, simply because there is no such thing as purely legal principles or purely criminological principles that, like platonic forms or ideas, are unassailable and that invisibly influence reality.

Ethos

If reality, as is argued here, is indeed multidimensional, then concrete examples will prove, more adequately than abstract theories, that serious research has to be trans-disciplinary. In the remainder I will therefore use a particular subject to illustrate why scientific disciplines should take each other's conclusions into account. Is there a better way, in a collection of contributions on the work of John Braithwaite, than by looking into what happens during restorative justice conferences? The dynamics that arise during those kind of conferences have repercussions that are relevant to several scientific aspects. The dynamics themselves, however, are neither ethical, nor purely psychological, nor purely legal. To grasp these dynamics I will use the concept ethos. 'Ethos' is an ancient Greek concept and, like all such concepts, it used to function before categories like the ethical and psychological became dominant. These concepts existed before our perception of reality was distorted by the scientific partition of property. Ethos enables us to trace the dynamics that are at play in restorative justice conferences, with regards to ethics, law, communication as well as group psychology repercussions. That is why we consider ethos a 'crossroads concept'.

The connection between ethos and ethics is well-known. After all, our modern concept of ethics derives from 'ethos'.[1] Aristotle uses 'ethos' in his *Ethica Nicomachea*, probably the most-quoted classical handbook of ethics. In this book, he describes how a lifestyle as citizen in a society can be excellent and appreciated and how such a lifestyle fits in with what people naturally pursue. Aristotle also uses the concept 'ethos' in his essay on rhetoric (1991) and his essay on literature (2001). These connections are less well known. In his *Rhetorics*, he states that if you want to inspire confidence in someone, it is not enough to merely communicate faultlessly, cleverly, smoothly, or with variations. You have to give the target audience the impression of being on their side by complying with what their 'ethos' requires. If you succeed in creating the perception that you are good in their eyes, whether you really are or pretend to be by complying with what their ethos requires, you will succeed in convincing them. If you speak like they do and start from the same implicit habits, presuppositions, and distinctions, the target audience will consider you one of them and accept your message more easily. If your discourse reveals you to depart from a different type of ethos, however, you will be considered an outsider. At that moment your message will no longer sound self-evident and your argumentation will seem 'unnatural'. In those circumstances, it will be much more difficult to get your message across. In his *Poetics*, Aristotle uses ethos as the collective term for various kinds of psychological dispositions like feelings, character traits, desires, expectations, vices, and virtues: in short, all kinds of psychological dispositions with the exception of logical reasoning. These dispositions can belong to a person but also to a group. He shows that an individual or group cannot just choose to be characterised by a certain 'ethos'. But it is in the

---

[1] 'Ethos' was later translated into Latin as 'mores', which refers to customs and habits. Our modern concepts of 'ethics' and 'morality' were derived from 'ethos' and 'mores'. However, the Romans were aware that the Greek 'ethos' had a broader meaning than 'mores' (Quintilianus 2001).

way that you make choices that your ethos is expressed (Aristotle 2001).[2] 'Ethos' is often translated as 'character' or 'habit'. It can refer to a person as well as a group. In Greek, 'doing something according to the ethos' means the same as 'doing something in a natural way'. Whoever respects the ethos is 'tactful' (Liddell and Scott 1996).

The concept 'ethos' brings up a reality that we take into account in daily practice but that we pay relatively little attention to. Everyone more or less knows what is meant when people talk about the mentality of an individual or group, but we seldom get around to taking into account this fact theoretically. The common approach to theory supposes that there are only individuals, that group emotions can be seen as the sum of individual emotions, and that public opinion is nothing but the average of what individuals think. These presuppositions are deceptive. Obviously, an ethos exists by the grace of the individuals who represent that ethos, but that does not alter the fact that an ethos in some way leads a life of its own. Let me expound on the reality an ethos relates to before looking at the context of the restorative justice conference by means of that central concept.

An ethos presupposes a characteristic way of interpreting. People who participate in the same ethos use a common conceptual framework. They use the same expressions and sayings. They base their judgement on the same distinctions and differences. They structure their perception based on parallel categories, which implies that they consider the same organisation of time and space and the same structured order of habits and customs self-evident. Because of their shared view on reality and their familiarity with the same social organisation, they inhabit the world in the same way. They cherish common expectations and ascribe the same privileges and duties to various positions.

Because the communication by means of which an ethos manifests itself does not only consist of verbal but also of non-verbal signs, an ethos not only shows itself intellectually but also in the domain of sensory perception. An ethos is, for instance, characterised by a specific intonation or a typical way of walking, moving, or gesticulating. The way of singing, laughing, or getting angry also corresponds to what is accepted within a particular mentality. Further, an understanding is externalised through a preference for certain forms and

---

[2] "Character [ethos] is that which reveals moral purpose, showing what kind of things a man chooses or avoids. Speeches therefore, which do not make this manifest, or in which the speaker does not chose or avoid anything whatever, are not expressive of character." *Op. cit.*, p. 64, (1450b).

colours and the appreciation of a specific cut or texture of clothing and what is shown and revealed by it. An ethos is also expressed in a preference for certain smells, rhythms, and music. An understanding of this kind not only exists in the head, but is incarnated in a physical style and tangible signs, for individuals as well as groups. An ethos is thus inscribed in the actual body and is therefore not easily changed. In that sense, an ethos corresponds with what Bourdieu (1988) called 'habitus'.

An ethos is also characterised by an emotional disposition or mood. This mood can show hopeful expectation, but can also be dejected. I can be combative or resigned, balanced or nervous. A group can be characterised by a strong self awareness, high self esteem and clear ideals, or conversely by insecurity, indecisiveness and low self esteem. The emotional aspect of an ethos is an indication of its vitality and motivation. The emotional appreciation of a group for a project adds to the appeal the project has to the individual. If the individual takes this project to heart he will be appreciated by the community, also when the individual finds the project important in itself. The public can give an individual heart that way. People who feel respected within the framework of an ethos often manage to excel and give their best. A group atmosphere can also be depressing and suffocating, however. Whoever is disapproved of or rejected within the framework of an ethos will have a very hard time holding up. An ethos generates respect for what a group deems important or considers forbidden. Durkheim, who considered these observations the corner stone of his sociological investigations, departed from the presupposition that the authority of social institutions and the sacredness of symbols derived from the affective unanimity within a group or community.

Precisely because the emotional support and rejection from an ethos are so impressive, people are often led by the dictates of the group. In other words, an ethos rarely creates an atmosphere entirely without obligations. Within an ethos, there is always behaviour that is expected or there are boundaries whose transgression is considered fundamentally wrong. People conform to what is required within an understanding. After all, nobody wants to experience the humiliation of being cast out by his group. That is why several philosophers, including Locke, have pointed out that the major guideline that people follow when it comes to morality is the law of fashion (Locke 1961). Peer pressure often operates inconspicuously. People seldom notice that what the group imposes is enforced, especially not when they sail with the wind. What corresponds to the requirements of the ethos often appears to go without saying and be entirely 'natural'. People often consider it 'normal' when they think and act in the way the group expects them to. They think that anyone who is in his right mind would spontaneously do so. The fewer people are aware of the particularity of their ethos, the more easily they will consider whatever is self-evident within their ethos as the behaviour that any right-minded world citizen should respect. Problems arise within an ethos when a perspective on another ethos grows.

The social control that an ethos generates presupposes that people can form an idea of what a group requires. People are in fact often quite capable of intuiting, based on small signs, a grin, or an involuntary movement, what a given group is thinking. In groups of people who are meeting for the first time and have 'not clicked' yet, it may be unclear what is thought, but in familiar groups, like a family, among colleagues, or even within the wider national community, individual members can often quite accurately assess what is expected. Studies have led to the conclusion that people can accurately predict in which direction public opinion is evolving (Noelle-Neumann 1993). It is as if people have a sixth sense that enables them to register what is 'in' or 'out'. They know which presidential candidate has gained 'momentum' and which candidate has messed up.

Liberal suspicion

There are lots of positive aspects to an ethos. It helps motivate people to live up to certain expectations and to take on certain projects that are appreciated by their group. An ethos creates vitality and self respect. People who make mistakes will only feel ashamed if they respect the ethos of their society. Only when there is an ethos can people be reconciled with their communities after a public confession and a ritual of penance. But an ethos also has very negative aspects. The moment the naturalness of an ethos is disrupted because an individual is capable of seeing reality from the perspective of another ethos, frictions may arise. The social pressure and public control can then become artificial and choke the freedom of the individual. An ethos infected by insecurity can motivate people to mercilessly slash at anything that threatens the group conformity. This is why group dynamics are curbed and ritualised in modern societies. Criminals are legally protected from popular fury. The public is represented by a public prosecutor and a jury. The public is not immediately given the floor. A trial aims at creating an objective and serene atmosphere, in which the rights of the defence are respected. Within the legal order, the individual is protected against rabble-rousing, popular fury, pressure of conformity, and mass hysterics. The judicial system can be considered a 'storm-free' space in which each party can speak out and the verdict is as impartial as possible.

Politically as well, the protection of individuals against any ethos is attempted by monopolising violence and granting the individual all kinds of liberties. A liberal democracy precludes any witch hunt and calls into account every group that imposes duties on individuals against their will. The major merit of liberalism is that it has been able to push back and curb the negative aspects of an ethos. Liberalism opposed the clerical interference of religious groups, fascist and communist ideologies, paternalism, elitism and any morality that denied individuals the right to decide for themselves how to develop their futures. The liberal resistance to every kind of ethos that obstructs individual freedom has grown over time into an alternative type of ethos: one of political correctness. Within this ethos every individual is expected to respect an atmosphere in which everyone can cultivate the opinion that his or her convictions, tastes and preferences are equal in value to the convictions, tastes and preferences of anyone else. The only limit to be respected is related to situations in which the expression of these convictions, tastes, and preferences would harm someone else.

The ethos of total equality as political correctness makes it hard to seriously discuss the moral and aesthetic value of tastes and preferences. It is a mentality that teaches that nothing sensible can be said on the importance of art, culture, and civilisation: you can only research whether a market exists for certain things. The liberal commitment to curbing the negative impact of the ethos has given the negative liberties a sacrosanct position but has simultaneously led to a certain anaemia. In liberal societies, anything people do seems all the same. Ethical and moral preferences are considered subjective, except for the procedural rules that, like traffic rules, make coexistence possible. In such a society, whose ethos aims at expelling ethos, guilt and reconciliation seem meaningless because there no longer appears to be a community beyond a collection of atomic individuals who each, in their own way, aim at the satisfaction of their personal liberties.

When legal proceedings become purely procedural and are completely detached from the ethos of a community, the judicial system can no longer function as an instrument of reconciliation. In such a society something like 'reintegrative shaming' becomes impossible. Of course things are never as bad as they seem. Even in communities that completely separate law and morality, group emotions play a part. But it remains a fact that when a community seems to become indifferent to what its members do, because it assumes that everyone has to be able to indulge his private desires without being troubled by social control, there is no room for reintegrative shaming.

The creation of an alternative ethos

The solution that John Braithwaite and Philip Pettit (1990) have proposed consists of a remarkable compromise. In *Not Just Deserts* they argue for a criminal law that is supported by citizens who collectively feel responsible for the continued existence of their dominion. The authors stress that a dominion does not only rest on 'objective' rights and liberties. Each dominion presupposes a shared commitment to, and trust in the fact that other people as well as the authorities will respect personal rights and liberties. As opposed to the liberal view, freedom in a dominion is considered a public good. The choice that is made in *Not Just Deserts* is original in this respect because, on the one hand, it connects with the liberal tradition and tries to protect individual rights against group ethos, but, on the other, it consciously tries to foster an alternative ethos by aiming for a shared sense of responsibility for the development and protection of liberties. It tries to cultivate an ethos to curb the dangers of the ethos. The difference between this republican ethos and the liberal ethos of political correctness allows for social control and for individuals as well as the community to grant themselves the right to morally reprimand other people when they do not meet their responsibility towards the common good. A transgressor should feel that the people around him disapprove of his behaviour and reprimand him for it. This is one of the aims of restorative justice conferences.

When this problem is analysed in the abstract, it seems relevant to foster an alternative ethos, but when looking at the particular context in which this ideal can be realised, things become less simple. I am afraid that when it comes down to organising a restorative justice conference, the appeal of the dominion will fall short, because it is limited to a commitment to, and a sense of, responsibility for negative liberties. In practice the organisation of conferences like these turns out to use other types of ethos than the one based on a shared respect for dominion. People will appeal to the family ethos, and invite friends and acquaintances, teachers and figures of authority from the neighbourhood. The ethos that is thereby introduced has far more 'guts' than the dominion ethos.

A dominion in itself cannot inspire. Enthusiasm for ideals of negative freedom is not enough. When you tell children to leave each other alone because they were pestering each other out of boredom, you may temporarily have ended the violence, but you have not addressed the boredom that caused it. Telling them to respect each other's freedom and physical integrity does not give them any ideas of what they should do in a positive sense. There is something embarrassing about the constant hammering away at negative freedom. It will not get us anywhere when we need a solution to riots in suburbs. Human rights cannot remedy a lack of positively valued projects that young people can appropriate to add a sense of value to their lives. The message that it is permissible, within the boundaries of the liberal state, to realise everything they want, is in itself not enough to create the feeling that there are things that are worth committing to. Respect for a dominion only makes sense when you are simultaneously convinced of the existence of positive projects to which you devote your life. The examples of colonists who created a dominion like Roger Williams on Rhode Island in 1644 illustrate that these people were not driven by liberties as such, but by the conviction that only if you are free can you authentically dedicate your life to your beliefs. Williams wanted to enable authentic religion. To him, freedom was not an aim in itself but a means. Besides creating liberties that everyone respects, within society also respect for art, science and culture will have to be ensured.

By way of conclusion

Every community wanting to increase a sense of responsibility for the dominion undoubtedly consists of different types of ethos that each correspond to a historical tradition. The authorities can found new institutions, organise conferences, and create rituals, but if the ethos that is to be fostered is not supported by existing traditions, social associations, labour unions, and churches, the idea of dominion will likely stay an ideal without a social basis. A criminologist wanting to contribute to better jurisdiction will therefore have to work out how to realise a responsible mentality, together with all kinds of different agencies. A major group of these is constituted by the media. There arc probably no instrumcnts with a morc obvious influcncc on thc cthos of society than the media. Their impact is underestimated because media are often considered as producers of products for individual users. Even though this is true in the end, the appeal of media products is that they enable individuals to keep in touch with the centre of public attention and the way in which events influence the ethos of society. The media put us in touch with the ethos, or rather, they transmit a partial image of the ethos and thus contribute to influencing it. If you want to foster a caring, nuanced, alert, merciful, and discerning ethos, you will therefore need to do more than carry through institutional legal reforms. Within the community, you will need to start a wide debate on which type of ethos you, together with all the other social participants, want to cultivate. This debate will inevitably have ethical, political, economic, and legal consequences.

This strategy seems complicated and naive. Bringing together so many different people seems impossible, which makes this approach less attractive. And since we as academics have the choice of pretending it is no concern of ours, we can withdraw into our own specialised fields of research.

Even though interdisciplinary research is a buzzword in many promising programme declarations, it remains a hard ideal to actualise. Many disciplines are guarded like private territories and are not accessible to unauthorised persons. This territorialism in academic circles is hard to temper and the field-specific fences are hard to break through. But after all, the only truthful option for any discipline is to turn towards the world – and there, everything that happens is intertwined.

References

Aristotle (2001) *Aristotle' Poetics*, F. Fergusson (intr.), S.H. Butcher (transl.), New York, Hill and Wang.

Aristotle (1991) *Aristotle 'On Rhetoric': A Theory of Civic Discourse*. Kennedy, George A. (ed.). New York/Oxford: Oxford University Press.

Pierre Bourdieu (1988) *Homo Academicus*, Cambridge, Polity Press / Oxford, Basil Blackwell.

John Braithwaite and Philip Pettit (1990) *Not Just Desserts: A Republican Theory of Criminal Justice* Oxford, UK: Clarendon Press.

Michel Foucault (1971) *L'ordre du discours*. Paris, Gallimard.

Harry Frankfurt (1988) *The Importance of What We Care About*. Cambridge, Cambridge University Press.

Immanuel Kant (1997) *Groundwork of the Metaphysics of Morals*. Mary Gregor, ed., Cambridge, Cambridge University Press.

H.G. Liddell and R. Scott (1996) *Greek-English Lexicon*, 9th edition, Oxford, Clarendon Press.

John Locke (1961) *An Essay Concerning Human Understanding*, J.W. Yolton (ed.), New York and London, Chapter 26, § 12.

John Stuart Mill (2002) *Utilitarianism*, 2nd ed., Ed. George Sher. Indianapolis: Hackett, Ch. 2, §1.

Elisabeth Noelle-Neumann (1993) *The Spiral of Silence: Public Opinion -- Our Social Skin*. Chicago, The University of Chicago Press.

Quintilianus (2001) *The Orator's Education,* Donald A. Russell (ed.), (Loeb Classical Library) Harvard, Harvard University Press, VI.2.8-9 & 13.

Bernard Williams (1993) *Ethics and the Limits of Philosophy*, London, Fontana Press.

OPPORTUNITIES AND DANGERS OF CAPITALIST CRIMINOLOGY

JOHN BRAITHWAITE

"I look upon Philosophy to be one of the most excellent Things in Nature, if used moderately."

> (The Colloquies of Erasmus ([1518] 1878) trans. N. Bailey, Vol 1, The Profane Feast, London: Reeves & Turner, p. 121; this was Erasmus's most famous work, published while he was at K.U.Leuven).

The boom market in criminology

I have been lucky in my professional life as a criminologist to be surrounded by so many good friends and insightful scholars. Among them are the authors of the fine papers in this volume, whom I thank. I enjoy their company. They typify why I have been so nourished by the community of scholars that is criminology. That is the positive way in which I think of criminology – as a community of interesting people who come together with common research interests on the topic of crime. I do not think of it as a discipline with methods and theories that are distinctive from the rest of the social sciences. Nevertheless, I have found theories I learnt from criminology most useful for understanding business regulation and the prevention of armed conflict.

I will argue here that criminology has been more a force for good than ill in the world. In some ways it deserves the astronomic growth we have seen in our lifetimes. Yet I have deep doubts about its evolution, just as I have about the discipline that gave birth to my abiding interest in criminology – sociology. Doubts about sociology are not the topic of this essay. Yet to understand why criminology has grown so fast in recent decades, while sociology has not, we must see how criminology has been parasitic upon sociology.

One of the greatest things undergraduates can get from a humanities education is what C. Wright Mills called a 'sociological imagination' (Mills 1959). A sociological imagination enables students to connect their individual experience to institutions and to their place in history. We learn to re-imagine our private troubles as public issues shaped within social structures. Note here that the 1970s boom in sociology, in turn, was in part parasitic on the discipline of history (via its appropriation of an historical imagination).

As a first and second year student, I found sociology difficult. In fact, I only scraped through with special permission to move on to second year sociology after an appeal of my grade. It was hard because the reading of classic sociology was so abstract. It became even more abstract with poststructuralist and postmodern critiques of the classics. The criminology courses taught within the sociology curriculum were a more benign environment for acquiring a sociological imagination and an historical imagination than sociological theory classes. Only after those concrete lessons did my sociological imagination motivate deep engagement with the classics and their critiques. I suspect my undergraduate experience was a common one. One of the reasons, then, that criminology has been a force for good is that it has been more successful in cultivating a sociological imagination than sociology itself. In the rich sociological imaginations manifest in this volume, we catch fine glimpses of how and why that promise has been realised by criminologists.

But what was it that attracted generations of young people like me to be (initially) so much more interested in crime than in Marx's transition from feudalism to capitalism to socialism or in Max Weber's protestant ethic and the spirit of capitalism? Ironically, it was capitalism. Markets for the sale of advertising on the mass media motivated journalists to sensationalise crime, to make it salacious, or simply to report it as a ripping yarn. It is these markets that drive the penal populism discussed by Lode Walgrave and Susanne Karstedt in this volume. When certain politicians then grasp the opportunity to harness this penal populism to their political projects, whether we admire or revile these politicians, crime becomes an even more fascinating topic to us. So we vote with our feet in markets for higher education, swelling criminology enrolments. And when we acquire enduring benefits from those classes, like a sociological and historical imagination, or a policy imagination for how to make the world a better place, or a critical imagination, we sometimes move on to higher degrees in criminology.

It seems like a benign story of the evolution of criminology as a major force in the social sciences. But criminology has succumbed to the very capitalist dynamics that gave it birth. First, because penal populism delivered its market power, in the market for higher education enrolments, temptations are rife to sacrifice the development of sociological, policy and critical imaginations on the altar of the fascinating narrative. Why bother with hard things like statistics and theory when the students are more titillated by a sociology of "nuts, sluts and perverts" (Liazos 1972)? Managerialists motivated by enrolments sadly sometimes find allies among critical theorists when they want to increase market appeal by trimming down statistics requirements, allies among policy criminologists when they trim the teaching of critical criminology. These capitalist market dynamics of dumbing down criminology education are rife.

Regulatory capitalism – more opportunities and dangers

Professional values in criminology could transcend these market dynamics were they not the only intellectual threat to the field. A common error is to think that the period of the rise of criminology as a discipline has been a period of the rise of neoliberalism. I take neoliberalism to be a set of discources and practices of privatisation and deregulation that increase the sway of markets and hollow out the state. Elsewhere I have argued (building on Jordana and Levi-Faur (2004), Levi-Faur (2004) and Vogel (1996)) that the world we have actually inhabited since the 1970s has not been characterised by neoliberalism, but by regulatory capitalism (Braithwaite 2008: Chapter 1). The dispensation of regulatory capitalism is, yes, the more vibrant markets part of neoliberalism, but coupled with growth in the size and interventionism of the state, a world of regulatory growth rather than deregulation.

Regulatory capitalism describes what has happened in the crime control industry. There has been much privatisation (and responsibilization) – in policing (Shearing and Stenning 1981), prisons (Harding 1997), and in dispute resolution through movements for mediation, restorative justice etc. At the same time state policing budgets and state interventionism, as manifest for example in imprisonment rates, have soared (Christie 1993; Garland 2001).

Regulatory capitalism also describes what has happened in the teaching of criminology. I have already argued that more vibrant market forces in higher education have allowed criminology to prevail over more abstract social sciecne disciplins in competition for students. But universities are not being deregulated. State regulation of universities motivated by the laudable goal of ensuring universities deliver more public value has increased. But so has private regulation by market entrepreneurs of the internet age. They market sales of "Good Universities Guides", ISI and Google Scholar citation counts, university rankings designed to increase sales of publications like the Times

Higher Education Supplement and the US News and World Report. Regulation by non-business, non-government organizations like professions is another important ingredient of regulatory capitalism. In the regulatory capitalism of Australian higher education, rankist organizations like the Academy of Social Sciences play important roles as servants of the regulatory ambitions of the state. Rankist organizations modelled on colonial traditions of blackballing by English gentlemen's clubs do their own private regulation by gate keeping admission to the upper echelons of the academy. Increasingly it is either difficult or impossible for a promising young criminologist to become a full professor without being admitted to membership of the Academy of Social Sciences. This is only one marker of the external regulation of quality. The aspiring professor must also attend to the external prestige and citation rankings of the places she publishes, for example. In Australia, the policy scientists have also captured the regulatory agenda through a formula that rewards universities (and therefore scholars) in proportion to the research grant funding dollars raised (mainly from the state and business).

The problem is not just the professional criminologists referred to by Ian Loader and Richard Sparks who capture the regulatory agenda through metrics like citation rankings of journals and policy criminologists who do so by valorizing grant dollars. Public criminologists have also captured regulatory metrics by persuading universities to count the times a scholar's name appears in the media. Like the valorizing of grant dollars, this strengthens the arm of criminology in competition with disciplines like philosophy, anthropology and history, as it is so easy for criminologists to get media hits with comments on the latest terrible crime, crime wave, or policy, especially in local media. Critical criminologists have not captured any of the metrics of regulatory capitalism in the academy. They have been too busy being critical and fighting factional wars for that; and so their influence in the criminological academy has waned since its highwater mark in the 1970s.

The regulatory metrics captured by the policy criminologists and public criminologists are inferior to rewarding scholars according to peer review of the distinctiveness and value of their contribution to learning. However, these forms of capture of regulatory capitalism by policy and public criminologists do not pose the deep danger of the capture of private and public regulation by metrics informed by the more entrenched forces of professional criminology. It is with these metrics where the deepest pathologies of regulatory capitalism – regulatory ritualism and gaming the metrics (Braithwaite, Makkai and Braithwaite 2007, Braithwaite 2008) – are given greatest scope. They cause people to publish in a place with higher prestige or with the right impact factor rather than in the place where the most relevant people will actually engage with the work. Hence, it is much better to publish a piece on crime in Pakistan in a second rate American journal than in the Pakistan Journal of Criminology, even if you are from Pakistan!

Naturally, market forces are shaped by the largest market for criminology, the United States. So professional metrics are hegemonically American (and Anglophone). Even within the US, metrics sustain the hegemony of capture by the professional criminology mainstream of the two most cited journals, *Criminology* and the *Journal of Quantitative Criminology*. In an American criminology or criminal justice program, you serve the competitive interests of your department poorly by being an interdisciplinary scholar who publishes in places other than criminology journals. This is a dead hand on the intellectual vitality of American criminology. In the very nation where market forces in education powered the greatest flowering of criminology, those same market forces have created metrics of regulatory capitalism that are profoundly destructive of intellectual innovation. Criminology was much more intellectually vibrant when it was in the process of emancipating itself from the disciplines of its former masters in sociology, psychology and law than today as an emancipated new discipline. As my mentor, Gil Geis, a former President of the American Society of Criminology put it: "Criminology [the journal] publishes increasingly statistically sophisticated articles on increasingly unimportant questions". Or as Bart Pattyn put it in his contribution to this volume, modern scholars "know precisely more and more about less and less."

If the same regulatory capitalism that fuelled the flowering of criminology is turning the garden barren, can we escape? Yes, the new rise of criminology in the 60 per cent of the world that is Asia cannot be fuelled by Anglophone regulatory metrics; Asia has a different philosophical heritage that puts reintegrative ideas on a more equal footing with punitive ones,[1] and has the potential to reinvigorate criminology in the course of this century. With the recent formation of the Asian Criminological Society, the ferment of ideas and the ascending excellence of Asian criminology is inspiring. Also inspiring is the quietly effective role Chinese criminologists have played in the dramatic reduction in resort to capital punishment in a China that until very recently

---

[1] Susanne Karstedt's Figures show 3 of the 4 largest Asian nations – India, Indonesia and Japan – count among 3 of the 4 nations with the lowest imprisonment rates in the world. China has a middling imprisonment rate.

accounted for 80 per cent of the world's executions, and the rise of evidence-based restorative justice there, including randomized controlled trials in eight Chinese cities led by a team from Beijing Normal University.

More fundamentally, at the end of the day the world university system rewards innovation and punishes the kind of stagnation that is inevitable from cultivating the mindless pursuit of quantitative indicators of excellence. Most good criminologists are not seduced by them. They use and market good performance against them when it comes their way to reap resources for their research teams. But most of the best criminologists have interdisciplinary interests and follow where ideas lead. They are more committed to the ideal of the university as a community of scholars from whom they draw cross-fertilization than they are to how they are measured as a criminologist.

Sparking criminology

Ian Loader and Richard Sparks agree that in the history of criminology so far there are more positive than negative things to say about it. Still, they too are critical. They also see the virtues of criminology that promotes sociological and historical imagination. They are more interested in interdisciplinary public social science than in public sociology or public criminology. Yet like Michael Burawoy, they see virtues to salvage, and complementarities in "professional", "policy", "critical" and "public" social science. Professional social science can give us rigorous theory and empirical methods; policy social science can help solve big problems of humankind; public social science can make scholars more democratically valuable as they engage in public dialogue with non-experts; critical social science interrogates the foundations of the other three discourses (and its own – it is reflexively critical) and helps us see the world through new lenses. At the same time, professional criminology can be so excessively committed to its discipline that it games markets and regulatory mechanisms in ways that debase the broader collegiality and excellence of universities. Policy criminology is very often servile to states that shamelessly exploit penal populism and shun thinking outside the box. Public criminologists can be embarrassing in the way they speculate wildly on sensational cases about which the evidence is yet to be sifted. And critical criminologists can be nihilistic, unworldly, sectarian, dogmatically unwilling to see the virtues of the other three traditions. Burawoy, Loader and Sparks are helpful in suggesting that we can nurture the strengths of these four kinds of social science and minimise their pathologies, especially their careerist pathologies, by putting them in creative tension at the level of ideas, as opposed to the level of gaming careers.

Lode Walgrave in this volume draws our attention to Sparks's (1997) use of Stones's (1996) distinction between "floaters" and "players". Players seek to be "useful" in solving policy problems. Floaters aspire to floating over the field, taking in its whole panorama, including the definition of the problems themselves. With homage to Richard Sparks, I would like to value "sparkers" above both players and floaters. The best scholars are rarely as wise, rarely as good at listening and adapting, as the best players of the policy process. Yet it seems such a waste if all they do is float. A good way for them to use their talents is to spark players with ideas, let the players play, then spark competing players when earlier sparks extinguish as embers. It's a collaborative contribution to a dialogue that connects to attempts at transformative change in which scholars have humility about their gifts as players. By not descending right down into the policy game, sparkers do continue to float, keeping a distanced perspective on the whole societal panorama. From above, they are not siloed as criminologists, but they can spark synapses that connect criminologists to economists, to demographers, to all the disciplines of the academy, and they can connect policy to professional to critical to public social science. Put another way, sparkers who float above the silos seem likely to add more intellectual, policy, critical and democratic deliberative value than scholars with an identity within a silo who virtuously network with scholars in other silos. But of course the latter is better than just being a professional or policy criminologist who rarely engages beyond other professional or policy criminologists.

Ethos and Justice

Bart Pattyn in his chapter sparks an interesting philosophical contribution to criminology. Reality, he argues, is so multidimensional that we cannot craft an ethical response to it without contextual wisdom, without understanding the history and customs within which ethical dilemmas arise and the symbols that express them. It follows that "serious research has to be trans-disciplinary".

Pattyn suggests the Aristotelean concept of ethos as a crossroads of insight. By ethos, he means common understandings, shared frames, but also partly what Clifford Shearing meant by "sensibility" (Shearing and Ericson 1991) – an ethos experienced at the individual level -- when Clifford described what was the best way to be productively effective in advancing some collective project, such as that of a research group. Clifford would say to friends that a good leader does not so much set down rules and guidelines, nor give detailed advice on what to do in a given situation; rather they cultivate shared sensibilities between them and those they would lead. Members of the team would then know what to do by enacting that acquired sensibility. In this spirit, Pattyn argues that Durkheim, like Aristotle, sees ethos as giving meaning, purpose and respect to group members who are able to make sense of it and enact it.

He sees modern justice systems as losing contact with the ethos of their communities. When they become no more than a set of rules and procedures, justice systems can no longer deliver reconciliation or reintegrative shaming. Yet procedural justice and rights are crucial protections against the potential tyrannies of an ethos. Pattyn generously sees the republican theory of criminal justice developed with Philip Pettit (Braithwaite and Pettit 1990) as an alternative justice ethos that takes seriously those crucial procedural and rights protections of the currently dominant liberal justice ethos. Yet it also involves the cultivation of a sensibility of sharing responsibility for the continuous improvement and protection of liberties. This project is about cultivating "Active responsibility" in communities, through restorative justice conferences, among other means, as opposed to a justice system that simply holds people passively responsible for what they have done in the past (Bovens 1998; Braithwaite and Roche 2000) or "earned redemption" (Bazemore 1999). Republicanism is an ethos of checks and balances against the dangers of ethos.

Pattyn's most important contribution is to argue that republican dominion, or freedom as non-domination (Pettit 1997), in itself cannot inspire. Nor can liberalism. When people suffer a grievance that leads them to respond with tactics of domination, they must be inspired with a concrete political program that can resolve that grievance. We can see restorative justice and other institutions of deliberative democracy as methods for discovering what those practical remedies are that might fit an extant ethos, and therefore inspire change. Restorative justice has an abstract political theory, but it also has a practical method for helping people, in concrete and local ways, to resolve their grievances.

Some people find a sense of value in their lives by campaigning for regulatory reforms to tackle climate change. Others do so by helping a victim of crime in their family to understand what they can do to feel safe again. Respect for dominion "only makes sense when you are simultaneously convinced of the existence of positive projects to which you devote your life" (Pattyn). Hence, for Pattyn the great republican projects, of the likes of Jefferson, inspired because republican freedom enabled the pursuit of more substantive (often spiritual and local community building) goals. This localism of objectives that charts practical solutions to peoples' problems which can inspire is why republican institutions are less invented in states like the United States and Germany, more in local communities like Virginia and Rhode Island (Pattyn's essay), Lubeck (Karstedt's), Florence, Bruges and Leuven.

Conceived this way, republican criminology and restorative justice actually seem less vulnerable to concerns about "evangelical" criminology than professional, policy or critical criminology fundamentalisms. Certainly, wide debate within a community about a shared ethos and an ethos of regulating the dangers of ethos will empower some to take an "evangelical" stand for say protecting victim rights. But it is not the deliberative, checked and balanced, evidence-based republican project that is evangelical. It is the concrete projects that some will be empowered to take up that sometimes will be dangerously evangelical, and therefore in need of critical scrutiny and concrete procedural checks.

Consumerism and the clinical

Lode Walgrave's paper shows why wide dialogue to discover a shared ethos of a community is so difficult in contemporary capitalism. We live in a world where politics has been marketized. This has had profound effects on criminology. Walgrave finds that citizens have declining trust in and insecurity about government. Decreasingly, they vote for the political program they think will be best for the nation; increasingly, they opt for the politician who will best serve their individual self-interest at the lowest price. Consumerist criminology he contends is more at the heart of this than is recognised by political scientists. Social institutions, including institutions of justice, are consumed. Walgrave has the interesting hypothesis that "perception of more and less safety is probably the nucleus of infection which gradually contaminates the overall quality of social life, civic commitments and democracy". Putnam's documented decline in social capital can be understood in terms of this rampant insecurity. A big part of this problem is that insecurity is marketed by actors who are selling a solution to it – law and order politicians, the police, the private security industry, even some criminologists and authors of murder mysteries, most of all the media.

Republican freedom as non-domination, like liberalism, in such structural conditions conduces to a world in which citizens exploit their rights to maximise their market advantages, hence Karstedt and Farrall's (2007) pathologies of everyday crimes of the middle classes. One of the things that feeds these pathologies is the increasing arrogance of the criminality of the masters of the universe within the bonus culture and the financial engineering culture that spread from Wall Street. Walgrave points out that globalization has put financiers in such a strong position that political leaders must be their servants if they want to survive, just as they must be servants of the opinion polls that reveal what political favours swinging voters most wish to consume. Political integrity is corrupted by capitalism from above and below (and from the middle). Yet the fact that fear of corporate crime that causes financial crashes is as much part of the insecurity discussed in Walgrave's paper as street crime reveals something of the contradictions that a republican criminology concerned with inequality and freedom from fear can prise open.

Tom Daems, in his contribution to this volume, goes beyond the challenges of a culture of control and a culture of consumerism to confront the culture of the clinical. He sees restorative justice as risking entrenchment of a clinical culture. Daems points to danger in the human condition of being a victim becoming primarily a clinical condition. Much restorative justice evaluation does oscillate between a consumerist logic (of measuring how satisfied victims and others are) and a therapeutic logic of how helped victims are, how much better they feel. Daems worries that a victim-oriented "therapeutization" of restorative justice might be incompatible with core values of the tradition such as active participation and reciprocal communication.

Post-Traumatic Stress symptoms are certainly of concern to we restorative justice scholars who see importance in Angel's (2005) finding that victims in cases randomly assigned to restorative justice have fewer symptoms. We should also see importance in investigating whether restorative justice increases post-traumatic growth in comparison to traditional criminal processes. When the restorative justice community acquires a balanced concern with both, then Daems' fears about a "therapeutization" of restorative justice might recede. Post-traumatic growth may be precisely about empowerment and participation, and therefore hardly at odds with restorative values. Traumatic victimization, like all setbacks, supplies an opportunity to grow. The imperative to transcend trauma triggers an opportunity for wider transcendence – of demands for enhanced control of others, of an existence of individualistic consumerism - in favour of civic engagement that can grow citizens into more caring, meaningful collective lives. We can be inspired by the extraordinary lives of survivors of war trauma like Sister Lorraine Garasu of Bougainville, who often spoke in our interviews of her peacebuilding leadership in the same frame as her personal recovery from trauma (Braithwaite *et al*. 2010).

Criminology doing its bit in bringing universities to the rescue

In an era when political integrity is almost universally sacrificed on the altar of a much more deeply capitalist culture than the world has ever seen before, one institution that can come into its own is the university. We have seen this great role many times throughout history. We saw it in massive movements against Western imperialism in all of the good universities of the US, Australia, New Zealand and France during the Vietnam War. We saw it with People Power that overthrew the Marcos dictatorship in the Philippines in 1986, in Poland, then right across the communist world during the 1980s to China in 1989. In the late 1990s we saw it in the student movement that played a crucial role in the overthrow of President Suharto. We see it today in West Papua with inspiring university-led resistance to Indonesian oppression. I have found it hard in returning from fieldwork in Indonesia to inspire my Australian students with stories of Indonesian students who massed in front of their university to prevent it from being burnt to the ground again (in Ambon) after it had just been rebuilt, actually standing in front of the tanks as they fired at the university buildings to destroy them. What is interesting to me is that both those Indonesian students and the military commanders ordering the tanks to fire understood so clearly the transformative significance of the ferment of ideas in universities.

Western universities in recent decades have become careerist places where inmates keep their heads down and seek to get ahead in the education market. We have seen that this is because universities are more ensnared today both by markets and by the regulatory steering of markets. It is no easy matter to break through this. Yet I am proud to say that criminology departments have often done that against the current. The exemplary role of university leaders in engaging with the social movement for restorative justice is an example, as is the role of academic criminologists in supporting unpopular prisoner rights movements, campaigns to reduce the use of imprisonment, campaigns to reduce capital punishment in China, campaigns against torture.

Universities should be places of free political ferment, places that argue about how normative theory should connect to explanatory theory,[2] as exemplified in the Pattyn and Walgrave contributions. My hypothesis is that when normative theory sparks explanatory theory, explanatory theory explains better; and when explanatory theory sparks normative theory, political theory makes more contextual sense and more meaningfully connects to the ethos of a people (Braithwaite and Pettit 2000). Yes universities should be places where a great deal of evangelism goes on. Those who warn against evangelism of course make important points about its dangers, but they must be careful that their prescriptions against evangelism can be even more dangerous for the health of universities. Universities should have Islamic student associations actively promoting jihad. What an indictment it is that in our universities today, students do this furtively, are cowed against doing so in open university forums. Universities are the best places to put this kind of evangelism out in the open because universities are the institutions best equipped for vigorous contestation of ideas. The upshot is that young Islamic students can come to believe in violent jihad without being exposed to the analyses of the best Islamic scholars who reason violence is a corruption of jihad. At the same time, non-Muslim inmates of our universities never learn from passing by the Islamist's loudhailer that for most Muslims jihad is a positive force in their lives in the same way that grace is in the spiritual lives of Christians.

How honoured I am to have received this honorary doctorate from the Katholieke Universiteit Leuven, where the reformation saw the scholarly evangelism of Erasmus help build one of the greatest universities of the sixteenth century, and helped teach Catholicism that there were important things to learn from the critiques of the Protestants. Leuven thus ultimately helped lay the foundations for a Europe where Catholics and Protestants would live in peace. My personal deep affection for Leuven as a university community of the 20th and 21st centuries arose because it was at the centre of laying new intellectual foundations for world peace, non-violence and non-domination through evidence-based restorative justice.

---

[2] Explanatory theories are defined here as ordered sets of propositions about the way the world is. Normative theories are ordered sets of propositions about the way the world ought to be.

Community and equality

In her chapter Susanne Karstedt takes up a theme shared with Walgrave and Pattyn when she invokes Herbert Mead's contention that laws should supply a vision of justice, capture the ethos and the imaginations of people, before they can govern. Karstedt also exemplifies the kind of sociological imagination that can be nourished by criminological research that is the starting point of this essay. She shows, cross-nationally, that the more individual autonomy is valued, the more egalitarian values are adopted, the better are prison conditions. Karstedt concludes that this is heartening news for the kind of republicanism Lode Walgrave (2008), Philip Pettit (1997), President Zapatero of Spain (Marti and Pettit 2010) and I have advanced. It is not quite so heartening, in my view, for the closely related kind of civic republicanism advanced by Cass Sunstein (1988), President Obama's "Regulation Czar", which prioritizes political equality but not economic equality.

At the same time, Karstedt's data throws down a challenge to the kind of republican criminology my colleagues and I have advanced. This challenge is also addressed in the writing of Pavlich (2001) and Walgrave (2008) on the dangers of certain kinds of communitarianism. Republican criminology has been Durkheimian in the sense of valorizing strong communities for enabling social control to work effectively and decently. It also valorizes republican checks and balances against abuses of collectivism. Karstedt's data shows that collectivism in national values is associated with worse prison conditions. How should we think about such results? It is early days with this cross-national values tradition of sociological criminology. Karstedt is a pioneer of it. So it is perhaps too early to rush to judgement on the challenge it poses to my kind of criminology. Yet here are my preliminary intuitions, shaped by reflecting on Karstedt's work over a number of years, and much influenced by earlier contributions such as Karstedt (2006).

The first thing I note is the paradox that the small scale societies from which I have learnt most about restorative justice, certain Melanesian and Polynesian societies with vibrant restorative traditions, are also societies with ferocious punitive traditions, warlike histories, with head hunting and cannibalism of enemies not uncommon. These societies vary greatly, but often use forms of indigenous justice that satisfy Western definitions of restorative justice for crime that occurs inside the village. This can work well in securing a low crime local society without prisons or much punishment, as I first concluded in 1969 when I lived in a village on Bougainville. Yet the strong collectivist identity of these societies can conduce to a contempt of the out-group, disrespect of them, and in times of tension, formidable willingness to humiliate and punish them.

I also learnt this in my experience of rugby league clubs as a young man. The more collective passion you have for the club, the more affection and forgiveness you experience toward your club mates, and the more venom and violence you are capable of directing at players from other clubs. Collectivism conduces to peace inside, violence outside. At the same time, I noticed how malleable these identities were. Changes of institutional frame were instantaneous when one was selected with players from those other hated clubs in a representative team. Within a more encompassing social structure, collective fellow-feeling with former enemies was quickly and palpably experienced. In Melanesia and Indonesia (Henley 2004), colonialism was often welcomed because it had the same effect. When church and colonial authorities insisted that more encompassing Christian and national identities trump traditional blood feuds between "tribes", there was often overnight embrace of former enemies and relief that the more encompassing structures of colonialism could adjudicate disputes that previously could only be settled by war. Resistance to the pacification of ancient enmities was frequently brief and weak.

In a completely different strand of Karstedt's work, we see this with reconciliation in post-World War II Europe (Karstedt 2004, 2009, 2010). Vindictive enemies did not take long to be reconciled warmly as allies. So my first hypothesis would be, yes, strongly collectivist values of an in-group conduce to punitiveness toward an out-group (as in these Karstedt data). But in-group boundaries can be readily expanded to embrace former out-groups. Then the former out-groups enjoy lower punitiveness than they would were they embraced by new comrades with a less strongly collectivist identity.

The problem is that late modern European legal traditions (common and civil law), that have utterly globalized in the last two centuries, conquering almost all the world's Buddhist, Islamic and animist legal systems (Wood 1997), persistently treat criminals as an out-group to be warehoused away from the in-group. Societies vary in where out-group boundaries are defined. So Japan is a society with strongly collectivist values and a willingness to treat most criminals who are dealt with by local police comparatively reintegratively. Yet when Japanese detectives take over from local police offenders who are not showing remorse, or when people are sent to prison, Japanese justice is highly stigmatizing (Miyazawa 1992; Braithwaite 2002: 18, 27), and includes recourse to capital punishment. That, I hypothesise, delivers Japan both a low crime rate and a low imprisonment rate, but with some deep problems in its justice system in terms of republican freedom. Still, for all its limits, this is one path to more republican justice – expanding the boundaries of the in-group of citizens who are seen as good people who occasionally err in doing bad things, and narrowing the boundaries of the out-group of bad people who are stigmatized. Diversion programs that reduce the number of offenders incarcerated are simple manifestations of this approach.

Restorative justice supplies a second path. It hands over criminals substantially to the care and adjudication of their in-group. And it works hard at finding or constructing an in-group for offenders who do not seem to have one. Moreover, restorative justice as a democratic praxis has a wider agenda of educating all citizens through the restorative justice experience to be more open to the benefits of rejecting stigmatization of out-groups. The experience of participating in a restorative justice conference does not always have that effect,[3] but it often does in comparison to the alternatives (Braithwaite 2002: 45-168). A social movement politics that succeeds in institutionalising restorative justice for dispute resolution among schoolchildren has some potential to help children learn to become reintegrative toward former enemies.

A third path is the one suggested by Bart Pattyn of a republican ethos of reproaching the excesses of ethos, a collective ethos of curbing the abuses of collectivism. It is a project of a transformative ethos, a justice system that supplies a different Meadian vision and inspiration for justice.

Conclusion

There are criminological floaters who are willing to get their hands dirty, sparkers! There are players who play dirty, as Walgrave puts it. There are evangelists like Erasmus who are trenchant critics of their own tradition. There are evangelists for science, evangelists against value-driven enquiry, who are closed-minded on the evidence for the devastating effect this has had on the quality of intellectual life in Western universities since the 1970s. As Walgrave argues, there are good and bad versions of all of the criminological

---

[3]   Nor do all versions of restorative justice even have these ambitions; for example, see Walgrave (2008) on how minimalist restorative justice options do not aspire to the republican ambitions under consideration here.

styles discussed in this volume. The sum of the encounters among them is always more valuable than the combination of what they could contribute separately. The genius of the university as an institution is that it makes collaboration across silos easier than it is for lawyers to collaborate with non-lawyers within an institution such as a court, economists with non-economists in a finance ministry, scientists with moral philosophers in a military nuclear research facility.

If universities have special competence in sparking transformative projects, they must be deeply engaged with the great value debates of politics and justice systems. Regulatory capitalism has created a golden era of sorts for criminology. This will turn to dross if market growth is the discipline's primary motivation; it will turn to dung if criminology continues to look inwards in relentless pursuit of performance metrics.

The path criminology can take is to show the whole university system a better way that is engaged collaboratively with other disciplines (and in dialogue with the democracy). It can help break the chains that regulatory capitalism has placed around universities. More vibrant markets for education deliver many good things (empowerment of students, more Eastern students on Western campuses) and so can regulation in sensible modalities like peer review. No field is better placed than criminology to reap the positive legacies of regulatory capitalism while transcending its pathologies, precisely because criminology is a boom discipline of regulatory capitalism.

For the moment, criminology is too comfortable with itself to see the potential to leave a great intellectual legacy. It is too much a creature of capitalism to turn around and bite it the way capitalism needs to be bitten. Universities have had bite at all of the critical junctures of modern history. Sadly criminology is more than ever a lap-dog of the capitalism and of the state that fattens it. Corporate crime scholarship has not grown in the way research on crimes of the poor has grown. Yet criminology could help solve some aspects of capitalism's deepest problems, like financial crises, that economics has failed to solve. Then it might capture a revered place in the history of science.

Criminology is unlikely to show the world how to create societies with low levels of predation and violence unless it is connected to a civil society politics of institutional transformation to end humiliation of out-groups and to progressively reduce inequality. That is the path to solving the problem of societies that suffer one kind of crime because certain classes exploit, other kinds because other classes are exploited (Braithwaite 1991). Arguing for "crime science" because nothing can be done about structural inequalities will not do. Criminology is unlikely to play its part in redeeming our failing universities without championing values of political freedom, political engagement, ferment, fearless exposure of the crimes of capitalism and evidence-based ways of fixing them. Societies that fix them will enjoy greater security, greater economic development and greater equality, avoiding the fate of Iceland. And the intellectual communities that help fix the crimes of capitalism will not suffer the busts that follow the booms of capitalism itself. For the moment, though, criminology is to capitalism what the spies of the inquisition were to Catholicism. Thankfully, Leuven is one place that might spawn criminology's Erasmus among is students.

References

Angel, C.M. 2005 *Crime Victims Meet their Offenders: Testing the Impact of Restorative Justice Conferences on Victims' Post-Traumatic Stress Symptoms*, Philadelphia: University of Pennsylvania, Unpublished PhD Dissertation in Nursing and Criminology.

Ahmed, Eliza, Nathan Harris, John Braithwaite and Valerie Braithwaite. 2001 *Shame Management through Reintegration*. Melbourne: Cambirdge University Press.

Bazemore, Gordon. 1999 "Communities, Victims, and Offender Rehabilitation: Restorative Justice and Earned Redemption." In *Civic Repentance*, edited by A. Etzioni. Lanham, Md: Rowman and Littlefield, pp. 45-96.

Bovens, Mark 1998 *The Quest for Responsibility*, Cambridge: Cambridge University Press.

Braithwaite, John 1991 "Poverty, Power, White-Collar Crime and the Paradoxes of Criminological Theory", *Australian and New Zealand Journal of Criminology* 24: 40-50.

Braithwaite, John 2002 *Restorative Justice and Responsive Regulation*. New York: Oxford University Press.

Braithwaite, John 2008 *Regulatory Capitalism: How it Works, Ideas for Making it Work Better*, Cheltenham: Edward Elgar.

Braithwaite, John, Hilary Charlesworth, Peter Reddy and Leah Dunn 2010 *Reconciliation and Architectures of Commitment: Sequencing peace in Bougainville*, Canberra: ANU E Press.

Braithwaite, John, Toni Makkai and Valerie Braithwaite 2007 *Regulating Aged Care: Ritualism and the New Pyramid*, Cheltenham: Edward Elgar.

Braithwaite, John and Philip Pettit 1990 *Not Just Deserts: A Republican Theory of Criminal Justice*. Oxford: Oxford University Press.

Braithwaite, John and Philip Pettit. 2000 "Republicanism and Restorative Justice: An Explanatory and Normative Connection." In *Restorative Justice: Philosophy to Practice*, edited by Heather Strang and John Braithwaite. Aldershot: Ashgate Dartmouth.

Braithwaite, John and Declan Roche. 2000 "Responsibility and Restorative Justice." Edited by M. Schiff and G. Bazemore (eds.), *Restorative Community Justice*, Cincinnati, Ohio: Anderson.

Braithwaite, John, Toni Makkai and Valerie Braithwaite 2007 *Regulating Aged Care: Ritualism and the New Pyramid*, Cheltenham: Edward Elgar.

Christie, Nils. 1993 *Crime Control as Industry: Towards Gulags, Western Style?* London: Routledge.

Garland, David 2001 *The Culture of Control: Crime and Social Order in Contemporary Society*. Oxford: Oxford University Press.

Harding, Richard W. 1997 *Private Prisons and Public Accountability*. Buckingham: Open University Press.

Henley, David 2004 "Conflict, justice, and the stranger-king indigenous roots of colonial rule in Indonesia and elsewhere", *Modern Asian Studies* 38(1): 85–144.

Jordana, Jacint and David Levi-Faur (eds) 2004 *The Politics of Regulation: Examining Regulatory Institutions and Instruments in the Governance Age*. Cheltenham: Edward Elgar.

Karstedt, Susanne 2005 *The Nuremberg Tribunal and German Society: International Justice and Local Judgment in Post-Conflict Reconstruction*, Paper to Asia Pacific Centre for Military Law Conference, Canberra: Australian National University.

Karstedt, Susanne 2006 "Democracy, values and violence: paradoxes, tensions, and comparative advantages of liberal inclusion", *Annals of the American Academy of Political and Social Science* 605: 50-81.

Karstedt, Susanne 2009 "The Endurance of Collective Memory: Germany 1950-1980", *Polish Sociological Review* 1 (165): 27-38.

Karstedt, Susanne 2010 "From Absence to Presence, from Silence to Voice: Victims in Transitional Justice since the Nuremberg Trials" *International Review of Victimology* 17 (1): 9-30.

Karstedt, Susanne & S. Farrall 2007 *Law Abiding Majority? The everyday crimes of the middle classes*. Briefing 3, July 2007, London: Centre for Crime and Justice Studies.

Liazos, A., 1972 "The Poverty of the Sociology of Deviance: Nuts, Sluts & Perverts", *Social Problems* 20(1): 103-120.

Marti, Jose Luis and Philip Pettit (eds.) 2010 *A Political Philosophy in Public Life: Civic Republicanism in Zapatero's Spain*, Princeton: Princeton University Press.

Mills, C. W., 1959 *The Sociological Imagination*, Oxford University Press, London.

Miyazawa, Setsuo. 1992 *Policing in Japan: A Study on Making Crime*. Albany, NY: State University of New York Press.

Pavlich, George 2001 "The Force of Community", in H. Strang and J. Braithwaite (eds), *Restorative Justice and Civil Society*, Cambridge: Cambridge University Press.

Pettit, Philip 1997 *Republicanism*. Oxford: Clarendon Press.

Shearing, Clifford and Richard V. Ericson 1991 'Culture as Figurative Action', *British Journal of Sociology* 42, (4): 481-506.

Shearing, Clifford and Philip Stenning. 1981 "Modern Private Security: Its Growth and Implications." In *Crime and Justice: An Annual Review of Research*, Vol. 3, edited by M. Tonry and N. Morris. Chicago: University of Chicago Press, pp. 193-245.

Sparks, Richard 1997 "Recent social theory and the study of crime and punishment", In *The Oxford Handbook of Criminology*, Oxford: Oxford University Press, 2nd: 409-435.

Stones, Rob 1996 *Sociological Reasoning* London: Palgrave-Macmillan.

Sunstein, Cass 1988 "Beyond the Republican Revival", *Yale Law Journal* 97: 1539-1590.

Vogel, Stephen K. 1996 *Freer Markets, More Rules: Regulatory Reform in Advanced Industrial Societies*. Ithaca and London: Cornell University Press.

Walgrave, L. 2008 *Restorative Justice, Self-Interest and Responsible Citizenship*, Cullompton (UK): Willan Publishing.

Wood, Philip R. 1997 *Maps of World Financial Law*. London: Allen and Overy.

SELECTED PUBLICATIONS BY JOHN BRAITHWAITE BY SUBJECT
(1979-2010, in ascending date order)

Criminological Theory

N. Shalhoub-Kevorkia & J. Braithwaite (2010) 'Victimology Between the Local and the Global', *International Review of Victimology* 17, 1-8.

S. Dinnen & J. Braithwaite (2009) 'Reinventing Policing Through the Prism of the Colonial Kiap', in Grabosky, Peter (ed.) *Community Policing and Peacekeeping*, CRC Press, Boca Raton, revised version of *Policing & Society*, 19(2):161-173, 2007.

E. Ahmed and J. Braithwaite, Shame, Pride and Workplace Bullying, in S. Karstedt, I. Loader and H. Strang (eds), *Emotions, Crime and Justice*, Oxford, Hart Publishing, forthcoming.

J. Braithwaite, V. Braithwaite and E. Ahmed, Reintegrative Shaming, in S. Henry and M. Lanier (eds), *The Essential Criminology Reader*, Boulder, Westview Press, 2005, 286-295.

J. Braithwaite, "What's Wrong with the Sociology of Punishment?", *Theoretical Criminology*, 7(1), 2003, 5-28. http://papers.ssrn.com/sol3/papers.cfm?abstract_id=319602

J. Braithwaite, "Transcontinental Migration of Convicts: A Contribution to the Sociology of Punishment" (Transkontinentale Migration von Strafgefangenen: Das Beispiel Australien), *Kölner Zeitschrift für Soziologie und Sozialpsychologie*, 43, 2003, 413-440.

J. Braithwaite, Domination, Quiescence and Crime, in S. Nagel (ed) *Policymaking and Peace: A Multinational Anthology*. Lexington, Mass.: Lexington Books, 2003.

E. Ahmed, N. Harris, J. Braithwaite and V. Braithwaite, *Shame Management Through Reintegration*, Melbourne, Cambridge University Press, 2001.

J. Braithwaite, "Crime in a Convict Republic", *The Modern Law Review*, 64(1), 2001, 11-50.

N. Harris and J. Braithwaite, Guilt, in N.J. Smelser and P. B. Baltes (eds) *International Encyclopedia of the Social and Behavioral Sciences*, Oxford: Pergamon, 2001, 6445-6448.

J. Braithwaite, "The New Regulatory State and the Transformation of Criminology", *British Journal of Criminology*, 40(2), 2000, 222-238.(Reprinted in D. Garland and R. Sparks (eds) Criminology and Social Theory, Oxford, Oxford University Press, 2000).

J. Braithwaite, "Shame and Criminal Justice", *Canadian Journal of Criminology*, 42 (3), 2000, 281-298.

J. Braithwaite, "Charles Tittle's *Control Balance* and criminological theory", *Theoretical Criminology*, 1997, 1(1), 77-97.

J. Braithwaite, Reintegrative Shaming, Republicanism and Policy, in H. Barlow (ed.), *Criminology and Public Policy: Putting Theory to Work*, Boulder: Westview Press, 1995.

J. Braithwaite, Inequality and Republican Criminology, in J. Hagan and R. Peterson (eds), *Crime and Inequality*, Palo Alto: Stanford University Press, 1995.

J. Braithwaite, "Beyond Positivism: Learning from Contextual Integrated Strategies", *Journal of Research in Crime and Delinquency*, 30, 1993, 383-99.

J. Braithwaite, "Pride in Criminological Dissensus", *Law and Social Inquiry*, 18, 1993, 501-12.

J. Braithwaite, "Shame and Modernity", *British Journal of Criminology*, 33, 1993, 1-18. (Reprinted in Parker, David, Rosamund Dalziell and Iain Wright (eds) Shame and the Modern Self, Australian Scholarly Publishing, Melbourne, 1996.)

B. Fisse and J. Braithwaite, *Corporations, Crime and Accountability*, Cambridge University Press, 1993.

J. Braithwaite, "Reducing the Crime Problem: A Not So Dismal Criminology", *Australian and New Zealand Journal of Criminology*, 25, 1992, 1-10.

J. Braithwaite, "Poverty, Power, White-Collar Crime and the Paradoxes of Criminological Theory", *Australian and New Zealand Journal of Criminology*, 24, 1991, 40-50. (Revised version reprinted in K. Schlegel and D. Weisburd (eds), White Collar Crime Reconsidered, 1992, Boston: Northeastern University Press. Unrevised version reprinted in M. McShane and F. Williams III (ed), Criminal Justice: Contemporary Literature in Theory and Practice, Hamden, ct.: Garland Publishing, 1997.)

J. Braithwaite, Preface, in R. Scheff and S. Retzinger, *Shame, Violence and Social Structure*, Lexington: Lexington Books, 1991.

J. Braithwaite and P. Pettit, *Not Just Deserts: A Republican Theory of Criminal Justice*, Oxford University Press, 1990.

J. Braithwaite and B. Fisse, "On the Plausibility of Corporate Crime Theory", *Advances in Criminological Theory*, 2, 1990, 15-38. (Reprinted in Japanese in Kokushikan Law Review, 1992, 15: 149-177) and also Reprinted in G. Geis, R.F. Meier and L. Salinger eds White-Collar Crime: Classic and Contemporary Views, 3rd Edition, New York Free Press).

J. Braithwaite, *Crime, Shame and Reintegration*, Cambridge University Press, 1989.

J. Braithwaite, "Criminological Theory and Organizational Crime", *Justice Quarterly*, 6, 1989, 333-358. (Reprinted in D Nelken (ed.) White Collar Crime, Aldershot: Dartmouth, 1994.)

J. Braithwaite, "The State of Criminology: Theoretical Decay or Renaissance", *Australian and New Zealand Journal of Criminology*, 22, 1989, 129-35. (Reprinted in Advances in Criminological Theory, Vol. 2, 1990, 155-166.)

J. Braithwaite, "Review Essay: The Mesomorphs Strike Back", *Australian and New Zealand Journal of Criminology*, 20, 1987, 45-53.

J. Braithwaite, Retributivism, Punishment and Privilege, in W.B. Groves and G. Newman, (eds), *Punishment and Privilege*, New York, Harrow and Heston, 1986. (Reprinted in R.G. Kasinsky (ed.) *Crime, Oppression and Inequality*, Needham Heights, MA, Ginn Press.)

J. Braithwaite, "Reply to Dr. Ernest van den Haag", *Journal of Criminal Law and Criminology*, 73, 1982, 790-93.

J. Braithwaite, Comment on "The Criminal Law as a Threat System", *Journal of Criminal Law and Criminology*, 73, 1982, 786-89.

J. Braithwaite, "Challenging Just Deserts: Punishing White-Collar Criminals", *Journal of Criminal Law and Criminology*, 73, 1982, 723-63.

J. Braithwaite and G. Geis, "On Theory and Action for Corporate Crime Control", *Crime and Delinquency*, April, 1982, 292-314. (Reprinted in part as "Stricter Penalties Would Reduce Corporate Crime", in Crime and Criminals: Opposing Viewpoints, 2nd ed. Edited by C. Debner, T. O'Neill and B. Szumski. St Paul: Greenhaven Press, 1984, 115-119; A. Duff (ed) Punishment. Aldershot: Dartmouth, 1993, 280-311; N. Shover and J.Wright (eds.), Crimes of Privilege: Readings in White-Collar Crime, New York, Oxford University Press, 2000).

J. Braithwaite, "The Myth of Social Class and Criminality Reconsidered", *American Sociological Review*, 1981, 46: 36-57. (Reprinted in J.F. Sheley (ed.) Exploring Crime, New York Wadworth Publishing Co, 1989.)

J. Braithwaite, "Merton's Theory of Crime and Differential Class Symbols of Success", *Crime and/et Justice*, 7/8, 1980, 90-94.

J. Braithwaite, *Inequality, Crime, and Public Policy*, London and Boston, Routledge & Kegan Paul, 1979. [Out of Print - Manuscript available in pdf]

Peacebuilding

J. Braithwaite, Hilary Charlesworth, Peter Reddy & L. Dunn (2010) *Reconciliation and Commitment: Sequencing Peace in Bougainville,* Canberra: ANU E Press.

J. Braithwaite, V. Braithwaite, M.Cookson & L. Dunn (2010) *Anomie and Violence: Non-truth and Reconciliation in Indonesian Peacebuilding,* Canberra: ANU E Press.

J. Braithwaite (2009) 'Conclusion: Hope and humility for weavers with international law', in B. Bowden, H. Charlesworth and J. Farrall (eds.), *The Role of International Law in Rebuilding Societies after Conflict: Great expectations*, Cambridge: Cambridge University Press, 270-289.

J. Braithwaite, Peacemaking Networks and Restorative Justice, in J. Flemming & J. Wood (eds), *Fighting Crime Together: The Challenges of Policing and Security Networks*, Sydney, UNSW Press, 2006, 195-217.

J. Braithwaite, Rape Shame and Pride: Address to Stockholm Criminology Symposium, 16 June 2006, *Journal of Scandinavian Studies in Criminology and Crime Prevention*, 7, 2006, 2-16. [note: this pdf is the submitted version only and may contain errors]

J. Braithwaite, "Pre-empting Terrorism", *Current Issues in Criminal Justice*, 17(1), 2005, 96-114.

J. Braithwaite, Domination, Quiescence and Crime, in S. Nagel (ed) *Policymaking and Peace: A Multinational Anthology*. Lexington, Mass.: Lexington Books, 2003.

J. Braithwaite, *Restorative Justice and Responsive Regulation*, New York, Oxford University Press, 2002.

J. Braithwaite, Thinking About the Structural Context of International Dispute Resolution, in M.R. Bustelo and P. Alston (eds) *Whose New World Order: What Role for the United Nations*? Sydney, Federation Press, 1991.

Republicanism

J. Braithwaite, "Shufukuteki Shihou" (Restorative Justice: Overview of the Concept), in Hosoi, Yoko, Nishimura, Haruo Kashimuri Shirou, and Tatsuno Bunri (eds), *Shufukuteki Shiho Sougouteki Kenkyu* (Restorative Justice: An Overview of Research) Tokyo , Kazamashobo, 24-34.

J. Braithwaite, "Families and the Republic", *Journal of Sociology and Social Welfare*, XXX1(1), 2004, 199-215.

J. Braithwaite, *Restorative Justice and Responsive Regulation*, New York, Oxford University Press, 2002.

J. Braithwaite, *Regulation, Crime, Freedom*. Aldershot: Dartmouth, 2000.

J. Braithwaite, Republican Theory and Crime Control, in K. Bussman and S. Karstedt (eds), *Social Dynamics of Crime and Control: New Theories for a World in Transition*. Oxford, Hart Publishing, 2000.

P. Pettit and J. Braithwaite, Republicanism and Restorative Justice: An Explanatory and Normative Connection, in H. Strang and J. Braithwaite (eds.), *Restorative Justice: From Philosophy to Practice*. Aldershot: Dartmouth, 2000.

J. Braithwaite and C. Parker, Restorative Justice is Republican Justice. In G. Bazemore and L. Walgrave (eds), *Restorative Juvenile Justice*. Palisades, New York: Criminal Justice Press, 1999.

J. Braithwaite, "On Speaking Softly and Carrying Big Sticks: Neglected Dimensions of a Republication Separation of Powers", *University of Toronto Law Journal*, 1997, 47, 305-361.

J. Braithwaite, "Community Values and Australian Jurisprudence", *Sydney Law Review*, 17, 1995, 351-72. (Reprinted in Chinese, Journal of Comparative Law, 1998, 13 (4), 361-377).

J. Braithwaite, "Reply: Broadening Disciplines that Dull as Well as Sharpen", *Sydney Law Review*, 17, 1995.

J. Braithwaite, Reintegrative Shaming, Republicanism and Policy, in H. Barlow (ed.), *Criminology and Public Policy: Putting Theory to Work*, Boulder: Westview Press, 1995.

J. Braithwaite, Inequality and Republican Criminology, in J. Hagan and R. Peterson (eds), *Crime and Inequality*, Palo Alto: Stanford University Press, 1995.

J. Braithwaite, Corporate Crime and Republication Criminological Praxis. In F. Pearce and L. Snider (eds), *Corporate Crime: Contemporary Debates*. Toronto: University of Toronto Press, 1995, 48-71. (Revised version in Nikon University Comparative Law Journal 11, 1994, 123-150.)

J. Braithwaite and P. Pettit, "Republican Criminology and Victim Advocacy", *Law and Society Review*, 28, 1994, 765-76.

P. Pettit, with J. Braithwaite, "The Three Rs of Republican Sentencing", *Current Issues in Criminal Justice*, 5, 1994, 318-325.

J. Braithwaite with P. Pettit, "Criminalization, Decriminalization and Republican Theory", *International Annals of Criminology*, 32 (1&2), 1994, 61-80.

B. Fisse and J. Braithwaite, *Corporations, Crime and Accountability*, Cambridge University Press, 1993.

P. Pettit, with J. Braithwaite, "Not Just Deserts Even in Sentencing", *Current Issues in Criminal Justice*, 1993, 4: 225-239. (Reprinted in *Revista Argentina Teoria Juridica* Volumen 7, 2007 as "No Solo Merecimiento, Aun al Sentenciar.")

I. Ayres and J. Braithwaite, Responsive Regulation: Transcending the Deregulation Debate, Oxford University Press, 1992.

J. Braithwaite, Good and Bad Police Services and How to Pick Them, in Peter Moir and Henk Eijkman (eds), *Policing Australia*, Melbourne: Macmillan, 1992.

J. Braithwaite and P. Pettit, *Not Just Deserts: A Republican Theory of Criminal Justice*, Oxford University Press, 1990.

Restorative Justice

J. Braithwaite, 'Restorative Justice', in H.J. Schneider (ed.), *International Handbook of Criminology*, Berlin, Walter de Gruyter, 2009.

J. Braithwaite, 'Restorative justice for banks through negative licensing', The British Journal of Criminology, 49(2), 2009, pp439-450.

J. Braithwaite, Building Legitimacy Through Restorative Justice, in T. Tyler (ed), *Legitimacy and Criminal Justice: International Perspectives*, Russell Sage, New York, 2007. pp 146-162.

J. Braithwaite, "Encourage Restorative Justice", *Criminology and Public Policy*, 6 (4), 2007, 689-696.

J. Braithwaite, Forward, in B. Morrision, *Restoring Safe School Communities*, Leichhardt, Federation Press, 2007, v.

J. Braithwaite, Restorative Justice, in H.J. Schneider (ed), *International Handbook of Criminology*, Berlin, Walter de Gruyter, forthcoming.

E. Ahmed and J. Braithwaite, Shame, Pride and Workplace Bullying, in S. Karstedt, I. Loader and H. Strang (eds), *Emotions, Crime and Justice*, Oxford, Hart Publishing, forthcoming.

J. Braithwaite, "Doing Justice Intelligently in Civil Society", *Journal of Social Issues*, 62(2), 2006, 397-407.

J. Braithwaite, "Narrative and "Compulsory Compassion"", *Law and Social Inquiry*, 31(2), 2006, 425-446.

J. Braithwaite, "Responsive Regulation and Developing Economies", *World Development*, 34(5), 2006, 884-898.

J. Braithwaite, Accountability and Responsibility Through Restorative Justice, in Michael Dowdle (ed), *Rethinking Public Accountability*, Cambridge University Press, 2006. [note: this pdf is the submitted version only and may contain errors]

J. Braithwaite, "Shufukuteki Shihou" (Restorative Justice: Overview of the Concept), in Hosoi, Yoko, Nishimura, Haruo Kashimuri Shirou, and Tatsuno Bunri (eds), *Shufukuteki Shiho Sougouteki Kenkyu* (Restorative Justice: An Overview of Research) Tokyo , Kazamashobo, 2006, 24-34.

J. Braithwaite, Peacemaking Networks and Restorative Justice, in J. Flemming & J. Wood (eds), *Fighting Crime Together: The Challenges of Policing and Security Networks*, Sydney, UNSW Press, 2006, 195-217.

J. Braithwaite, "Between Proportionality and Impunity: Confrontation => Truth => Prevention, The American Society of Criminology 2004 Sutherland Address", *Criminology*, 43(2), 2005, 283-306. (Reprinted in C. Slakmon, Machado & P. Bottini (eds), *Novas Direções no Governança da Justiça e da Segurança (New Directions in the Governance of Justice and Security)*, Brasília-D.F.: Ministry of Justice of Brazil, United Nations Development Programme – Brazil & the School of Law of the Getulio Vargas Foundation – São Paulo, 2006, 371-388.) (Reprinted in *Revista Argentina Teoria Juridica* Volumen 7, 2007 as "Entre la Proporcionalidad y la Impunidad")

E. Ahmed and J. Braithwaite, "Forgiveness, Shaming, Shame, and Bullying", *Australian and New Zealand Journal of Criminology* , 38(3), 2005, 298-323.

J. Braithwaite, E. Ahmed and V. Braithwaite, Shame, Restorative Justice and Crime, in F. Cullen, J. Wright and K. Belvins (eds), Taking Stock: The Status of Criminological Theory, *Advances in Criminological Theory*, 15, 2005, 397-417.

J. Braithwaite, "Families and the Republic", *Journal of Sociology and Social Welfare*, XXX1(1), 2004, 199-215.

J. Braithwaite, "Emancipation and Hope", *The Annals of the American Academy of Political and Social Science,* 592, March 2004, 79-99. (Reprinted in C. Slakmon, Machado & P. Bottini (eds), *Novas Direções no Governança da Justiça e da Segurança (New Directions in the Governance of Justice and Security)*, Brasília-D.F.: Ministry of Justice of Brazil, United Nations Development Programme – Brazil & the School of Law of the Getulio Vargas Foundation – São Paulo, 2006, 389-410)

N. Harris, L. Walgrave and J. Braithwaite, "Emotional Dynamics in Restorative Conferences", *Theoretical Criminology*, 8(2), 2004, 191-210.

J. Braithwaite, "Restorative Justice and De-Professionalization", *The Good Society* 13(1), 2004, 28-31.

J. Braithwaite, "Holism, Justice and Atonement", *Utah Law Review*, 2003(1), 389-412.

J. Braithwaite, Principles of Restorative Justice, in A. von Hirsch, J.V. Roberts, A.E. Bottoms, K. Roach and M. Schiff (eds) *Restorative Justice and Criminal Justice: Competing or Reconcilable Paradigms?*. Hart Publishing, Oxford, 2003, 1-20.

J. Braithwaite, Domination, Quiescence and Crime, in S. Nagel (ed) *Policymaking and Peace: A Multinational Anthology*. Lexington, Mass.: Lexington Books, 2003.

J. Braithwaite, Restorative Justice and Corporate Regulation, in Elmar G.M. Weitekamp and Hans-Jürgen Kerner (eds). *Restorative Justice in Context. International Practice and Directions*, Willan Publishing, Devon, UK, 2003, 161-172.

J. Braithwaite, Does Restorative Justice Work? In Gerry Johnstone (ed), *A Restorative Justice Reader: Texts, Sources, Context*. Willan Publishing, Devon, UK, 2003, 320-352.

J. Braithwaite, *Restorative Justice and Responsive Regulation*, New York, Oxford University Press, 2002.

H. Strang and J. Braithwaite (eds), *Restorative Justice and Family Violence*, Melbourne, Cambridge University Press, 2002.

J. Braithwaite, "Setting Standards for Restorative Justice", *British Journal of Criminology*, 42(3), 2002, 563-577.

J. Braithwaite, "Restorative Justice and Therapeutic Jurisprudence", *Criminal Law Bulletin*, 38(2), 2002, 244-262.

J. Braithwaite, "Restorativna I reaktivna u cilju uspostavljanja mira u svetu", *Temida*, 2(4), 2002, 3-28.

J. Braithwaite, and H. Strang, Restorative Justice and Family Violence, in H. Strang and J. Braithwaite (eds), *Restorative Justice and Family Violence*. Cambridge University Press, Cambridge, 2002.

J. Braithwaite, In Search of Restorative Jurisprudence, in L. Walgrave (ed.), *Restorative Justice and the Law*. Collompton, Devon: Willan Publishing, 2002.

J. Braithwaite, Linking Crime Prevention to Restorative Justice, in J. Perry (ed.), *Restorative Justice: Repairing Communities Through Restorative Justice*. Lanham, Md.: American Correctional Association, 2002.

J. Braithwaite, Restorative Justice, in P. Bean (ed.) *Crime: Critical Concepts in Sociology*. London: Routledge, 2002.

E. Ahmed, N. Harris, J. Braithwaite and V. Braithwaite, *Shame Management Through Reintegration*, Melbourne, Cambridge University Press, 2001.

H. Strang and J. Braithwaite (eds), *Restorative Justice and Civil Society*, Melbourne, Cambridge University Press, 2001.

J. Braithwaite, "Crime in a Convict Republic", *The Modern Law Review*, 64(1), 2001, 11-50.

J. Braithwaite, "Youth Development Circles", *Oxford Review of Education*, 27(2), 2001, 239-252.

J. Braithwaite, "Restorative Justice and a New Criminal Law of Substance Abuse", *Youth and Society*, 33(2), 2001, 227-248.

J. Braithwaite, Intention Versus Reactive Fault, in N. Naffine, R. Owens and J. Williams (eds), *Intention in Law and Philosophy*. Ashgate-Dartmouth, Aldershot, 2001.

J. Braithwaite, Reconciling Models: Balancing Regulation, Standards and Principles of Restorative Justice Practice, in H. Mika and K. McEvoy (eds), *International Perspectives on Restorative Justice Conference Repor* t. Queen's University, Belfast, 2001.

J. Braithwaite, and D. Roche, Responsibility and Restorative Justice, in G. Bazemore and M. Schiff (eds), *Restorative Community Justice: Repairing Harm and Transforming Communities*. Anderson Publishing Co., Cincinnati, 2001.

H. Strang and J. Braithwaite (eds), *Restorative Justice: Philosophy to Practice*, Aldershot, Dartmouth, 2000.

J. Braithwaite, "Survey Article: Repentance Rituals and Restorative Justice", *Journal of Political Philosophy*, 8(1), 2000, 115-131.

J. Braithwaite, "Shame and Criminal Justice", *Canadian Journal of Criminology*, 42 (3), 2000, 281-298.

J. Braithwaite , "Restorative Justice and Social Justice", *Saskatchewan Law Review*, 63(1), 2000, 185-194. (Reprinted in E. McLaughlin, R. Fergusson, G. Hughes and L. Westmorland (eds) Restorative Justice: Critical Issues. London:Sage, 2003).

J. Braithwaite, "Decomposing a Holistic Vision of Restorative Justice", *Contemporary Justice Review*, 3(4), 2000, 433-440.

J. Braithwaite, Democracy, Community and Problem Solving, in G. Burford. and J. Hudson (eds), *Family Group Conferencing: New Directions in Community-Centered Child and Family Practice*. New York, Aldine de Gruyther, 2000.

J. Braithwaite, "Restorative Justice: Assessing Optimistic and Pessimistic Accounts", *Crime and Justice: A Review of Research*, Vol. 25 (ed. M. Tonry), 1999, 1-127.

L. Walgrave and J. Braithwaite, "Guilt, Shame and Restoration", *Justitiele Verkenningen*, 1999, 25 (5), 71-80.

J. Braithwaite, "A Future Where Punishment is Marginalized: Realistic or Utopian?" *UCLA Law Review*, 1999, 46 (6), 1727-1750.

J. Braithwaite and C. Parker, Restorative Justice is Republican Justice. In G. Bazemore and L. Walgrave (eds), *Restorative Juvenile Justice*. Palisades, New York: Criminal Justice Press, 1999.

J. Braithwaite, Education, "Truth, Reconciliation: Comment on Scheff", *Revista Juridica Universidad de Puerto Rico*, 67(3), 1998, 609-614.

J. Braithwaite, Restorative Justice, in M. Tonry (ed), *The Handbook of Crime and Punishment*. New York: Oxford University Press, 1998, 323-344.

J. Braithwaite, "Conferencing and Plurality", *British Journal of Criminology*, 1997, 37(4), 502-506.

J. Braithwaite, "Commentary: law, morality and restorative justice", *European Journal on Criminal Policy and Research*, 1997, 5(1), 93-98.

J. Braithwaite, "Searching for Epistemologically Plural Criminology (And Finding Some)", *Australian and New Zealand Journal of Criminology*, 29(2), 1996, 142-146.

J. Braithwaite, "Restorative Justice and a Better Future", *The Dalhousie Review*, 76(1), 1996, 9-32. (Reprinted in E. McLaughlin, R. Fergusson, G. Hughes and L. Westmorland (eds) Restorative Justice: Critical Issues. London:Sage, 2003).

J. Braithwaite, Resolving Crime in the Community: Restorative Justice Reforms in New Zealand and Australia, in C. Martin (ed.), *Resolving Crime in the Community Mediation in Criminal Justice*, London: Institute for the Study and Treatment of Delinquency, 1995.

J. Braithwaite, Diversion, Reintegrative Shaming and Republican Criminology. In Günter Albrecht and Wolfgang Ludwig-Mayerhofer (eds), *Diversion and Informal Social Control*, Berlin: Walter de Gruyter, 1995. 141-158.

J. Braithwaite, Restorative Justice. F.W.M. McElrea (ed.), *Re-thinking Criminal Justice vol 1. Justice in the Community*. Auckland: Legal Research Foundation, 1995.

J. Braithwaite, "Applying Some Lessons from Japanese and Maori Culture to the Reintegrative Shaming of Criminal Offenders", *Japanese Journal of Criminal Psychology*, 32, 1994, 181-96.

J. Braithwaite and S. Mugford, "Conditions of Successful Reintegration Ceremonies: Dealing with Juvenile Offenders", *British Journal of Criminology*, 34, 1994, 139-171. (Reprinted in D. Karp (ed.), Community Justice: An Emerging Field. New York: Rowman and Littlefield, 1998 Reprinted in K. Laster, Law as Culture, Sydney: Federation Press.)

J. Braithwaite and K. Daly, Masculinities, Violence and Communitarian Control, in T. Newburn and B. Stanko (eds), *Just Boys Doing Business*, London: Routledge, 1994. (Reprinted in M. Valverde, L. MacLeod and K. Johnson eds., *Wife Assault and the Canadian Criminal Justice System*, 1995, and translated to Servian in *Temida*, 4(2) 2002: 29-44).

J. Braithwaite, Thinking Harder About Democratizing Social Control, in C. Alder and J. Wundersitz, (eds) *Family Conferencing and Juvenile Justice: The Way Forward or Misplaced Optimism?* Canberra: Australian Institute of Criminology, 1994.

J. Braithwaite, What Is to be Done about Criminal Justice? in B. Brown and F. McElrea (eds) *The Yough Council in New Zealand: A New Model of Justice*, Auckland: Legal Research Foundation, 1993.

J. Braithwaite, "Reducing the Crime Problem: A Not So Dismal Criminology", *Australian and New Zealand Journal of Criminology*, 25, 1995, 1-10.

J. Braithwaite, *Crime, Shame and Reintegration*, Cambridge University Press, 1989.

ABOUT THE AUTHORS

Ivo Aertsen is Professor of Criminology at the K.U.Leuven (Belgium). He holds degrees of psychology and law from the same university. His main fields of research and teaching are Victimology, Penology and Restorative Justice. Within the Leuven Institute of Criminology, he co-ordinates the Research Line on Restorative Justice. Dr. Aertsen has been chair of the European Forum for Restorative Justice from 2000-2004, and has co-ordinated COST Action A21 on Restorative Justice research in Europe from 2002-2006. He is Editorial Board member of several journals and is involved in various practice and policy oriented partnerships, both at the national and international level. In 2010 he received the first European Restorative Justice Award of the European Forum for Restorative Justice. (www.law.kuleuven.be/linc)

John Braithwaite studied sociology at the University of Queensland. He is an Australian Research Council Federation Fellow and Founder of RegNet (the Regulatory Institutions Network) at the Australian National University. In the past he has worked on a variety of areas of business regulation and on the crime problem. His best known work is on the ideas of responsive regulation and restorative justice. In recent years he has embarked on a 20-year comparative project called *Peacebuilding Compared*, with various co-authors. John Braithwaite has been active in social movement politics around these and other ideas for 40 years in Australia and internationally. His book *Regulatory Capitalism: How it works, ideas for making it work better* (2008) summarizes many of those developments. He was the recipient of the 2006 Stockholm Prize in Criminology, as well as of various honorary awards. (www.anu.edu.au/fellows)

Tom Daems studied (European) criminology and political science at the K.U.Leuven (Belgium) and the London School of Economics (U.K.). At this moment he is a Postdoctoral Fellow from the Research Foundation Flanders (FWO) at the Department of Criminal Law and Criminology, K.U.Leuven. He is the author of *Making Sense of Penal Change* (Oxford University Press, 2008) and *De bestraffingssociologie van David W. Garland* (Boom Legal Publishers, 2009). He is also a co-editor of *Institutionalizing restorative justice* (Willan, 2006) and five other volumes (published in Dutch) dealing with the work of Zygmunt Bauman, criminology, electronic monitoring, imprisonment and punitiveness in Belgium. In 2009 he was awarded the

Willem Nagel Prize of the Dutch Society of Criminology and the Denis Carroll Prize of the International Society for Criminology for his book *Making Sense of Penal Change*. (www.law.kuleuven.be/linc)

Susanne Karstedt is Professor of Criminology and Criminal Justice at the Centre for Criminal Justice Studies, University of Leeds. Before, she held a Chair in Criminology at Keele University, where she moved from Germany in 2000. Her research and writing focuses on cross-cultural and international criminology, in particular on democratic values and institutions, and she has a track record of research and publications on transitional justice. She is a member of the editorial boards of several international journals and has (co-) edited books and special issues on a range of topics. Among her publications figure *Legal Institutions and Collective Memories* (2009), *Democracy, Crime and Justice* (edited with G. LaFree, 2006) and *Emotions, Crime and Justice* (edited with I. Loader and H. Strang, 2011). In 2007 Susanne Karstedt was awarded the Thorsten Sellin & Sheldon and Eleanor Glueck Award by the American Society of Criminology. (www.law.leeds.ac.uk)

Ian Loader is Professor of Criminology and Director of the Centre for Criminology at the University of Oxford (U.K.). Ian is author of various books, including *Youth, Policing and Democracy* (1996, Palgrave), *Policing and the Condition of England: Memory, Politics and Culture* (2003, Oxford, with A. Mulcahy), *Civilizing Security* (2007, Cambridge, with N. Walker) and *Public Criminology?* (2010, Routledge, with R. Sparks). He is currently working on a book on the consumption of security and continues to research and write about the relationship between crime, punishment and democratic politics. Ian is an Editor of the *British Journal of Criminology* and the Associate Editor of *Theoretical Criminology*. He currently chairs the Research Advisory Group of the Howard League for Penal Reform. From time to time he writes columns for *The Guardian* and makes other contributions to public debate about crime and justice. (www.crim.ox.ac.uk)

Jeroen Maesschalck studied Public Administration and Philosophy at the U.Ghent (Belgium) and at the London School of Economics and Political Science. He holds a Ph.D. in Social Sciences from the K.U.Leuven (Belgium). He is currently associate professor at the K.U.Leuven, where he serves as the Director of the Leuven Institute of Criminology. He is also Research Fellow in Integrity of Governance at the Free University of Amsterdam and co-chair of the Study Group on Ethics and Integrity of Governance of the European Group of Public Administration (EGPA). His teaching and research interests lie in the fields of public administration ethics and of management and policy-making in the criminal justice system. He also teaches qualitative research methods.(www.law.kuleuven.be/linc)

Letizia Paoli is full professor of criminology at the K.U.Leuven Faculty of Law (Belgium). Italian by birth, she received her Ph.D. in social and political sciences from the European University Institute in Florence in 1997, after studying political sciences at the University of Florence and at Georgetown University in Washington, DC. From 1998 to 2006, she was a senior research fellow at the Max Planck Institute for Foreign and International Criminal Law in Freiburg, Germany. She also served as consultant to the Italian Ministries of the Interior and Justice, and the UN Office for Drug Control and Crime Prevention (UNODCCP, now UNODC) and the UN Interregional Crime and Justice Research Institute (UNICRI). Since the early 1990s she has published extensively on the Italian mafia, organised crime, drugs and related control policies. (www.law.kuleuven.be/linc)

Stephan Parmentier studied law and sociology at the K.U.Leuven (Belgium) and sociology and conflict resolution at the University of Minnesota-Twin Cities (U.S.A.). He currently teaches sociology of crime, law, and human rights at the Faculty of Law of the K.U.Leuven, and has served as the head of its Department of Criminal Law and Criminology (2005-2009). He was appointed in 2010 as the Secretary-General of the International Society for Criminology and currently also serves on the Advisory Board of the Oxford Centre for Criminology and the International Institute for Sociology of Law (Oñati) Board. His research and publications relate to human rights violations in situations of violent conflict, strategies and mechanisms for justice and peace building, and quality management in the administration of criminal justice. (www.law.kuleuven.be/linc)

Bart Pattyn studied theology and philosophy at the K.U.Leuven (Belgium). He currently teaches ethics at the K.U.Leuven and is editor-in-chief of *Ethical Perspectives*, an international journal which promotes the dialogue between fundamental and applied ethics. He is director of the Centre of Ethics at K.U.Leuven and member of the board of *Metaforum*, an institution that promotes interdisciplinary dialogue within this university. (www.kuleuven.be/oce)

Richard Sparks is Professor of Criminology and Director of Research in Law at the University of Edinburgh and Co-Director of the Scottish Centre for Crime and Justice Research (all U.K.). His main research interests lie in the sociology of punishment (especially imprisonment); penal politics; public responses to crime and punishment; and the uses, abuses and non-uses of criminological knowledge in shaping public policy on crime and punishment. His current work, in collaboration with Ian Loader (University of Oxford), concerns the competing claims of autonomy and advocacy in crime and justice research, and the place of criminology in debates on the public roles of the social sciences, published in their book *Public Criminology?* (Routledge, 2010). Other publications include: co-author (with Evi Girling and Ian Loader) of *Crime and Social Change in Middle England* (2000), co-editor (with David Garland) of *Criminology and Social Theory* (2000) and (with Tim Hope) of *Crime, Risk and Insecurity* (2000). He is a member of the editorial boards of several journals including *Punishment & Society*, of which he was editor-in-chief 2000-2004. (www.law.ed.ac.uk)

Lode Walgrave is Emeritus Professor of Criminology at the K.U.Leuven (Belgium), where he directed the Research Group of Youth Criminology. He has been a founding member and chair of the *International Network for Research on Restorative Justice* and of the *International Association for Criminology of Youth*. The vast majority of his publications deal with youth offending, youth justice and restorative justice. Among the main titles published in English are (1999) *Restorative Juvenile Justice. Repairing the Harm of Youth Crime* (with Gordon Bazemore as co-editor), (2004) Restoration in Youth Justice (in M. Tonry and A. Doob (eds.), *Youth Crime and Youth Justice. Comparative and Cross National Perspectives)*, (2008) Criminology as I see it ideally. Address delivered on the occasion of his receipt of the 2008 European Criminology Award (*Newsletter of the European Society of Criminology*), (2008) *Restorative Justice, Self Interest and Responsible Citizenship*. In 2008, Lode Walgrave received the ESC *European Criminology Award*. (www.law. kuleuven.be/linc)

About the series *Society, Crime and Criminal Justice (Samenleving, Criminaliteit en strafrechtspleging)*

The Sparking Discipline of Criminology is volume 35 in the series *Society, Crime and Criminal Justice*.

Series Editors: I. Aertsen, S. Bogaerts, J. Goethals, F. Hutsebaut, J. Maesschalck, L. Paoli, S. Parmentier, S. Pleysier, J. Put, B. Spriet, D. Van Daele, F. Verbruggen, R. Verstraeten, G. Vervaeke

Still available in the series:

Het beleid van de jeugdmagistraat
Franssens Marieke, Put Johan, Deklerck Johan,
ISBN 978905867827, 2010, paperback, 352 p.,
Nederlands, *Samenleving, Criminaliteit en Strafrechtspleging* 34

Elektronisch toezicht
De virtuele gevangenis als reële oplossing?
De Decker Stef, Daems Tom, Robert Luc, Verbruggen Frank (red.),
ISBN 9789058677808, 2009, paperback, 192 p. , Nederlands,
Samenleving, Criminaliteit en Strafrechtspleging 33

Gerechtelijke geestelijke gezondheidszorg: wetenschap, beleid en praktijk
Liber Amicorum Joris Casselman, Goethals Johan,
Hutsebaut Frank, Vervaeke Geert (red.),
ISBN 9789058675163, 2005, paperback, 426 p., Nederlands,
Samenleving, Criminaliteit en Strafrechtspleging 32

Strafrecht als roeping
Liber amicorum Lieven Dupont, Spriet Bart, Van Daele Dirk,
Verbruggen Frank, Verstraeten Raf (red.),
ISBN 9789058674876, 2005, paperback, V-1268 p., Nederlands,
Samenleving, Criminaliteit en Strafrechtspleging 31 a+b

De verjaring van de strafvordering voor rechtspractici
Verbruggen Frank, Verstraeten Raf (red.)
ISBN 9789058674784, 2005, paperback, 226 p., Nederlands,
Samenleving, Criminaliteit en Strafrechtspleging 30

Tussen klassieke en moderne criminele politiek
Leven en beleid van Jules Lejeune, Christiaensen Stef
ISBN 9789058673640, 2004, paperback, 746 p., Nederlands,
Samenleving, Criminaliteit en Strafrechtspleging 28

The Impact of World War II on Policing in North-West Europe
Fijnaut Cyrille (ed.)
ISBN 9789058673541, 2004, paperback, x-184 p., English
Society, Crime and Criminal Justice 27

Legaliteit en rechtsvinding in het strafrecht
Een grondslagentheoretische benadering, Claes Erik
ISBN 9789058672926, 2003, paperback, 522 p., Nederlands
Samenleving, Criminaliteit en Strafrechtspleging 24

Victim policies and criminal justice on the road to restorative justice
A collection of essays in honour of Tony Peters,
Fattah Ezzat, Parmentier Stephan (eds)
9789058671813, 2001, paperback, 460 p., English,
Society, Crime and Criminal Justice 23

Victim-Offender Mediation in Europe
Making Restorative Justice Work, The European Forum
for Victim-Offender Mediation -(ed.)
ISBN 9789058670359, 2000, paperback, 382 p., English,
Society, Crime and Criminal Justice 20

On Punishment
The Confrontation of Suicide in Old-Europe
Vandekerckhove Lieven
ISBN 9789058670243, 2000, paperback, 182 p., English,
Society, Crime and Criminal Justice 19

Support for Crime Victims in a Comparative Perspective
A Collection of Essays Dedicated to the Memory of Prof. Frederic McClintock,
Fattah Ezzat, Peters Tony (eds)
ISBN 9789061869276, 1998, paperback, 256 p., English,
Society, Crime and Criminal Justice 13

Restorative Justice for Juveniles
*Potentialities Risks and Problems for Research. A selection of papers presented
at the international conference Leuven May 12-14 1997*, Walgrave Lode (ed.)
ISBN 9789061869207, 1998, paperback, 408 p., English,
Society, Crime and Criminal Justice 12

About
LEUVEN UNIVERSITY PRESS

Leuven University Press, established in 1971 under the auspices of Katholieke Universiteit Leuven, is an ambitious academic press of international standing.

Today the press has over a thousand books in print, in a broad range of fields including music, art & theory, text & literature, history & archaeology, philosophy & religion, society, law & economics.

All LUP publications are published with care and attention to detail. Prior to publication, all manuscripts are assessed by an independent editorial board and external specialist readers to ensure the highest academic standards. Combined with a service-oriented and personal this peer review process defines our publishing policy.

In the USA and Canada all English-language titles are distributed and sold through Cornell University Press. In the UK, Ireland, Denmark, Sweden, Norway, Finland, France, and Greece Leuven University Press is represented by University Presses Marketing and the titles are distributed by NBN International. In the Netherlands, all titles are available via Centraal Boekhuis. In addition to this international network of distributors, booksellers, and library suppliers, Leuven University Press makes use of digital distribution options such as Google Books, Amazon.com, and other e-book platforms to promote and market LUP titles.

Leuven University Press is a full member of the Association of American University Presses and a founding member of the Association of European University Presses.

Visit the website www.lup.be **for more information about the titles and publishing policy of Leuven University Press.**

Contact

Leuven University Press
Minderbroedersstraat 4, box 5602
3000 Leuven
Belgium
T   +32 (0)16 32 53 45
F   +32 (0) 16 32 53 52
E   info@upers.kuleuven.be
W   www.lup.be

Ordering information

Individuals
• All Leuven University Press publications are available from your local bookshop or can be ordered directly by mail, fax, or e-mail at info@upers.kuleuven.be or online at www.lup.be.

Bookshops and libraries
• Orders may be sent by mail, fax, or e-mail to info@upers.kuleuven.be.
Belgian bookshops can also order through boekenbank.be.

Customers in the Netherlands
• Bookshops in the Netherlands can order through Centraal Boekhuis www.centraalboekhuis.nl.

Customers in North America and Canada
• All English-language publications of Leuven University Press are available through Cornell University Press:
Cornell University Press Services
PO Box 6525, 750 Cascadilla Street,
Ithaca, NY 14851
USA
Phone: 1-607-277-2211
Fax: 1-607-277-6292
E-mail: orderbook@cupserv.org

Sales Representation in UK, Ireland, Denmark, Sweden,
Norway, Finland, France, and Greece
• University Presses Marketing
The Tobacco Factory
Raleigh Rd. Southville
Bristol, BS3 1TF, United Kingdom
Phone: +44 117 902 0275
Fax: ++44 117 902 0294
E-mail: sales@universitypressesmarketing.co.uk
http://www.universitypressesmarketing.co.uk/

Customers in UK, Ireland, Denmark, Sweden, Norway and Finland

• NBN International

Order Department

10 Thornbury Rd.

Plymouth, PL6 7PP, United Kingdom

Phone: +44 1752 202301

Fax: +44 1752 202333

E-mail: orders@nbninternational.com

http://www.nbninternational.com/